CW01671786

SHERSTON: THE CITY OF WHITE WALLS

Cover: View of Sherston High Street, c 1910.

Above: View at the junction of Tanner's Hill (left) and Grove Road (right). 'Topper' Thompson pushing his bike followed by daughter Josephine.

Below: Approaching Sherston from Malmesbury, Styles and Miles' shop on the right of the Easton Town crossroads, 1915.

SHERSTON

The City of White Walls

A VILLAGE HISTORY

Cilla Liddington

Published in 1996 by
Cilla Liddington
37 High Street
Sherston
Wiltshire

Design and typesetting by
EX LIBRIS PRESS
1 The Shambles
Bradford on Avon
Wiltshire
BA15 1JS

Typeset in 11 point Bookman

Printed and bound by Cromwell Press
Broughton Gifford, Wiltshire

ISBN 0 9528603 0 9

CONTENTS

TRADES & COMMERCE

PUBLIC HOUSES

BUILDINGS & SITES OF INTEREST

ACKNOWLEDGEMENTS

My thanks go to everyone in Sherston who has helped and encouraged me in my researches. Their generous contributions of memories and photographs form a major part of this book, and have helped turn an idea into a reality.

Special thanks go to my father, Gordon Sainsbury, for recounting his early memories of life growing up in Sherston; Mr & Mrs Harry Butler; Jane Thomas for her encouragement and help; the late Reverend Walter Page, who left a notebook filled with village history, which was a constant point of reference and kept me on track.

Thanks are also due to the County Hall in Trowbridge, Chippenham Library, and Malmesbury Library; the County Council's mobile library service has proved an ideal place to catch unsuspecting Sherstonians on a Friday morning; to Michael Marshman, Head of Local Studies at Trowbridge, Pamela Slocombe in the Wiltshire Buildings Record Office, Trowbridge; to Phil Bishop for reproducing part of the 1840 Tithe map; to Lin Prior for not only typing the manuscript but also putting my work in order, and without whose professional skills this book would not have been produced; and to Bill Tullberg for checking the manuscript; and to the following for allowing their treasured photographs to be included: Richard Aggett, Miss Dora Ball, Miss Kitty Ball, Mrs Emmy Blanchard, Joan Butler, Mr & Mrs Leonard Butler, Dorothy Compton, Kath Evans, Pam Forster, Lionel Glass, June Godwin, Pat Goodall, Doug Goulding, Mary Goulding, John Jobbins, Mike Kniveton, Tony Mills, Rachel Moody, Mr & Mrs Harry Neal, Mr & Mrs Stan Neal, Violet Neal, Arthur Palmer, Wendy Payne, Michael Poole, Bill Pritchard, Mr & Mrs Ron Purnell, Mr & Mrs Philip Saunders, Kath Skingley, Valerie Smith, George Stephens, Miss Stinchcombe, Sam Thompson, Mr & Mrs Tony Thompson, Major AJ Turnor, John Waite, Dave & Pat Walsh and Daphne White.

Last, but certainly not least, a very special *thank you* to my husband, Alan, and my children, Max, Gary and Tamara, all of whom have been a constant source of help and encouragement over the last two and a half years.

Sherston

I have always determined that, should my book ever be published, I would dedicate it to my mother, Margaret (Peggy) Sainsbury, 1927-76. This photograph of my mother and father was taken in 1946.

PREFACE

Several of my friends have asked me why I wanted to attempt to write a book about Sherston. There are several reasons, but the most important one to me is that I have always loved this village – the village where I was born, grew up, and I hope never to leave. I have traced my ancestry in the village to the late seventeenth century and have a strong sense of *belonging*.

Most of my research for this book has been provided by talking and listening to the older generation of Sherstonians, who would reminisce with me about their lives growing up in Sherston. Most of these memories are of happy times, but there are of course those of sadder occasions.

Whilst talking to these friends, I was surprised to learn that in the village from 1920 to the 50s there were approximately sixty shops and businesses, and it was my interest in learning more about these that started my research. I was delighted to discover that there is a wealth of memorabilia kept safely in drawers and albums, a lot of which I have been privileged to reproduce in this book.

My hope is that all who read the book will enjoy its photographs and maybe find old friends and relatives amongst them. I have attempted to be as accurate as possible in putting names to faces. However, memories are fallible and for any inaccuracies, I apologise.

In this book of photographs and memories, I hope to show what a special place Sherston was – and still is.

Cilla Liddington
May 1996

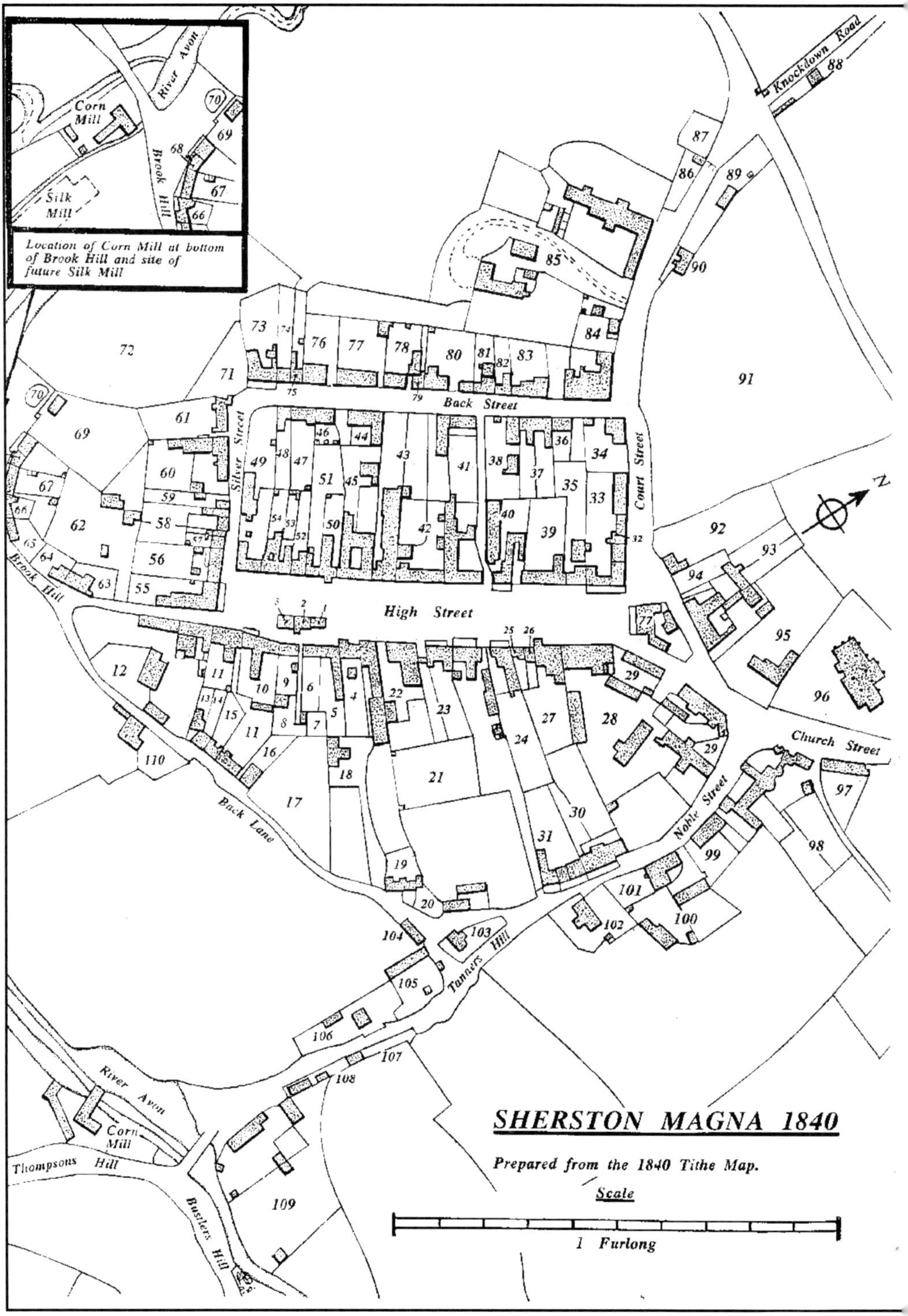

SHERSTON MAGNA 1840

Prepared from the 1840 Tithe Map.

SHERSTON MAGNA TITHES' LIST FOR 1840

No.	Property	Owner	Occupier
1	Tolsey building	Sarah Cresswell	Edward Jobbins
2	House and garden	William Dickenson	William Dickenson
3	"	Thomas Deverall	Mary Berry
4	"	Edward Jobbins	Edward Jobbins
5	"	James Stiles	James Stiles
6	"	Hannah Lewis	William Palmer
7	"	J. Window & W. Taylor	Mary Drew
8	"	Roger Gauntlett	Sarah Goslett
9	"	John Hacker	Joseph Wilcox
10	"	Samuel Manning	Nathaniel Compton
11	"	Robert Davis Little	George Snell
12	"	Edward Lyne	James Elsip
13	"	Richard Sherbourne	Thomas Neal
14	"	Thomas Rice	Thomas Rice
15	"	Thomas Thompson	William Sherbourne
16	"	Roger Gauntlett	Samuel Stubbing
17	Garden	William Palmer	William Palmer
18	House, garden & yard	William Amos	William Amos
19	House and garden	John Jones	Francis Evans
20	"	George Cresswell	Ethelbert Neal
21	House, garden & yard	John Henry Howell	Henry Holborow
22	House and garden	William Palmer	John Dickenson
23	"	Edward Boulton	Roger Gauntlett
24	"	Henry William Howell	Luke Cox
25	"	Ann Curtis	Ann Curtis
26	"	Thomas Deverall	William Wilcox
27	"	Samuel Manning	Thomas Thompson
28	Parsonage, barn etc.	Dean & Chapter of Gloucester	William Sainsbury
29	Rattlebone Inn	T Luce, Dean & Chapter Glos.	Thomas Bridgman
30	House and garden	William Lewis	William Lewis
31	"	Richard Gregory	Richard Gregory
32	"	William Wise	Robert Gifford
33	"	Robert Davis Little	John Prior
34	"	Jonah Hayes	Jonah Hayes
35	"	Edith Harry	Edith Harry
36	"	Mary Marsh	William Neal
37	"	Church land (church wardens)	Mary Evans
38	"	Thomas Deverall	Thomas Deverall
39	"	Church land (church wardens)	William Merchant
40	"	Edward Boulton	John Lyne
41	Swan Inn and garden	Edward Boulton	Solomon Gough
42	Angel Inn and garden	William Ody	Thomas Rice
43	Malthouse and garden	Samuel Manning	
44	Meeting House	John Prior	John Prior
45	House, garden & yard	Thomas Collingbourne	Moses Higgs
46	House and garden	William Wicks	William Wicks
47	"	Hillier Neal	Hillier Neal
48	"	Mary Butler	Philip Shewring
49	"	Sarah Cresswell	Edward Purnell
50	"	John Chapman	Edward Wilcox
51	"	William Palmer	William Neal
52	"	Joseph Lewis	Joseph Lewis
53	"	William Morris	William Morris
54	"	Henry William Howell	Ann Higgs
55	"	William Sainsbury	William Sainsbury
56	"	William Liddiard	William Liddiard
57	"	Thomas Rice	Thomas Rice

No.	Property	Owner	Occupier
58	House and garden	David Rice	David Rice
59	Yard and garden	Ethelbert Howell	Ethelbert Howell
60	House, garden & malthouse	Ethelbert Howell	Ethelbert Howell
61	House and garden	John Kimery	George Cook
62	"	Alexander Rice	John Bishop
63	"	Thomas Deverall	Isaac Pearce
64	"	Richard Gregory	William Neal
65	"	Joseph Curnock	James Neal
66	"	Edward Rice	John Neal
67	"	John Rice	John Rice
68	"	William Harris	Robert Pinner
69	"	Henry William Howell	Thomas Palmer
70	Garden on waste	Henry William Howell	Daniel Palmer
71	House and garden	George Cresswell	William Wise
72	Rabbit warren	George Cresswell	Charles Sysum
73	House and garden	Ethelbert Howell	Richard Skeats
74	"	Thomas Evans	
75	"	William Lewis	William Lewis
76	"	Sarah Cresswell	John Evans
77	Barn, yard etc.	Samuel Manning	
78	House and garden	Samuel Manning	William Drew
79	"	Thomas Neal	Cyrenous Berry
80	"	Joseph Hughes	William Bishop
81	"	Hillier Neal	Hillier Neal
82	"	George Rice	George Rice
83	"	James Bailey	James Bailey
84	"	Mary Watts	Mary Watts
85	House, garden & yard	George Cresswell	Charles Sysum
86	House and garden	John Cook (Commissioner of Turnpike roads)	Charles Drew
87	Village Pound	Richard Estcourt Cresswell	
88	House and garden	R.S. Holford	Charles Andrews
89	"	Sarah Cresswell	John Golding
90	"	William Wicks	John Rice
91	Pennymead	Sarah Cresswell	Rev Charles Whitcombe
92	House and garden	Sarah Cresswell	William Palmer
93	"	Hiram Wicks	Hiram Wicks
94	"	Samuel Manning	James Moreton
95	Vicarage house	Rev Charles Whitcombe	
96	Church & churchyard	Rev Charles Whitcombe	
97	House and garden	Joseph Partridge	William Smokeham
98	"	Sarah Cresswell	Thomas Neal
99	"	George Cresswell	Thomas Mince
100	Yard and building	T.T. & E. Coxwell	William Sainsbury
101	House and garden	R.S. Holford	Daniel Shewring
102	House and yard	George Cresswell	James Neal
103	"	George Cresswell	Thomas Sherbourne
104	Stables & cart house	George Cresswell	William Amos
105	House and garden	Thomas Deddles	Thomas Neal
106	"	Edward Gregory	Estcourt Gregory
107	Garden on waste	Edward Gregory	Estcourt Gregory
108	House and garden	George Reeves	William Jobbins
109	House, garden & Skin Yard	Thomas Clarke (Fellmongers)	Robert Clarke
110	Barn, yards etc.	J. Window & W. Taylor	

Lord of the Manor	Richard Estcourt Cresswell
Churchwardens	Edward Rice and Daniel Holbrow (care of church lands)

Over 700 numbered properties appear on the Tithe map, held at County Hall, Trowbridge. All arable land, orchards, pastures, and woodlands of Sherston Magna are included.

HISTORY

1 Sherston: The City of White Walls

The ancient name of Sherston was *Dreff Wenn*, and the village is located in the north-west corner of Wiltshire. The first mention of Sherston, or *Scorranstone*, was made by Ethelred who was Ealdorman of Mercia in the 9th century, Mercia being the centre of Britain.

The Romans almost certainly inhabited the village as the Fosseway is just two miles away. Also the remains of ancient Roman earthworks, consisting of rampart and ditch, were found in the field known as the Pennymead, now the recreation ground. Also traces of a large Roman villa, built in approximately 350AD, were found in a field just outside the village.

In 1016 King Canute came with a great army. The Saxons were led by King Edmund Ironside, and by his side was John of Sherston, whose surname became Rattlebone, possibly due to the lusty blows he dealt with his sword. John was captain of the local militia. The men of the village would be called to fight for king and country by the sound of a trumpet, blown from Bustlers Hill.

Over two days a fierce and bloody battle supposedly took place on the hills either side of the Cliff. At the end of the second day Canute broke camp and retreated back to London. At the same time, John received a dreadful wound, but to enable him to carry on fighting to the end, he clasped a stone tile to the wound to stop his guts from spilling.

For generations the children of Sherston were taught these lines:

"Fight well Rattlebone,
Thou shalt have Sherstone."
"What shall I with Sherstone doe,
Without I have all belongs thereto?"

"Thou shalt have Wyck and Willesly,
Easton Towne and Pinkeney."

To this day, Rattlebone remains the village hero, with the Rattlebone Inn named in his honour.

Sherston's wide main High Street was the site where the weekly market took place, but in 1511 a terrible fire destroyed the main part of the village. However, some evidence of its antiquity still remains.

Although the market was discontinued after the fire, Sherston was still an important town. There is in existence at least one Tradesman's Token, about the size of a 20p piece. It has on one side *Thomas Davis in Shuston Magnae 1651*, and on the reverse the veiled head of the Blessed Virgin Mary, which was the stamp of the Mercers' Company.

Up until the early part of the century, village life saw little change. Sherston in particular was a very close knit community. Everything a person needed was in the village – work, leisure, entertainment, shops – in fact, there was little cause to leave the village. When motorised transport became more popular things slowly began to change, with people losing their dependence on the village.

As well as the passing on of old Sherstonians, also gone are the ancient names and titles of lands and properties. Who now knows the location of Hockerhille, the Charcoal Gardens, Oxleaze, the Walnut Ground, Austin's Mead, and the King's Gardens? These were all listed in the rates' books dating from 1884.

In 1871 the population of Sherston was 1,588 including the hamlet of Willesley. In 1991 this number had dropped to 1,370, despite there being 300 more houses in the village.

Opposite above: Approaching the village of Sherston Magna from the Luckington Road, c. 1935.

Opposite below: Extract from Kelly's Trade Directory, 1895, listing businesses in Sherston.

SHERSTON MAGNA (or Great Sherston) is a village and parish, on the river Avon, 5½ miles west-by-south from Malmesbury terminal station on a branch of the Great Western railway and about 5½ south-west from Tetbury, in the North Western division of the county, Chippenham hundred, Malmesbury union, petty sessional division and county court district, rural deanery of Malmesbury, archdeaconry of Bristol and diocese of Gloucester and Bristol. The church of the Holy Trinity is a fine old structure, in the 13th century Gothic style, having chancel, nave of six bays and aisles, and a south porch, with square embattled tower in the centre with 5 bells and a clock, and contains a few memorials: there are 490 sittings. The register dates from the year 1653. The living is a vicarage, with Sherston Parva, or Pinkney, annexed, average tithe rent-charge £76, joint gross yearly value £300, net £254, with 6 acres of glebe land, with residence, in the gift of the Dean and Chapter of Gloucester, and held since 1884 by the Rev. East Frederick Thomas Ribbans B.A. of Trinity College, Dublin. There are one Congregational, two Baptist and one Primitive Methodist chapels. There is a reading room with about 50 volumes. Here is a silk ribbon manufactory. There are charities of about £13 annual value for the benefit of the poor. R. E. Cresswell esq. is lord of the manor, and Capt. George Holford of Weston Birt, Gloucestershire, and Colonel Wyatt William Turnor are the principal landowners. The soil is brashy; subsoil, gravel. The chief crops are wheat, barley and roots. The area of the parish is 3,773 acres; rateable value, £5,427; the population in 1891 was 1,349, including the hamlet of Willesley, 2 miles north.

Parish Clerk, Robert Purnell.

Post, M. O. & T. O., S. B., Express Delivery & Annuity & Insurance Office.—Harry Dicks, sub-postmaster. Letters arrive by mail cart from Malmesbury at 7.30 a.m; dispatched at 6.10 p.m. in winter & 6.40 p.m. in summer

Schools.

British (mixed), built in 1840, for 120 children; average attendance, 73; W. J. Seldon, master

National (mixed), to hold 150 children; average attendance, 135; George Dear, master

Carrier.—Ralph Golding, to Chippenham, mon. & fri. returns same day; Yate, station, thurs.; Tetbury, wed

Davis Francis Arthur, Lady's wood
Evans Mrs. Thomas
Harry Mrs. Sandpits
Knapp Mrs
Neale Benjamin Thomas Mills
Parsons Edward
Ribbans Rev. East Frederick Thomas B.A. (vicar), Vicarage
Rice Edmund
Silcox Rev. Geo. P. (Congregational)
Thompson Miss
Tolerton William Ratcliffe M.D., M.Ch

COMMERCIAL.

Andrews Elizabeth (Miss), draper
Berry Ann (Mrs.), farmer
Berry Nathaniel, shopkeeper
Berry William, fishmonger
Bishop Maurice, fishmonger
Blackford Richard, farmer
Boulton Alfred, plumber & glazier
Boulton Mrs. Jane, tobacconist
Brain Mrs. Amelia, farmer, Widlays
Bridgeman Cornelius, farmer
Brooks Benjamin, machinist
Camm Francis, boot maker
Causton Edwin, pig dealer
Clark John, fellmonger
Clark William, fellmonger
Cook Alfred, shopkeeper
Darling Daniel A. & Co. silk & cotton manufacturers (Alfd. Lister, man)
Dicks & Sons, drapers & grocers Post office
Elford James shopkeeper
Elford Joseph, tinplate worker
Elsip Chas. frmr. Easton Town farm
Elsip Thomas, baker
Evans Thomas, miller (water)
Evans William, shoe maker
Evans William, fishmonger
Eyres William, farmer
Ford Andrew & Son, tailors
Fruen Henry, beer retailer & carrier
Goodfield Samuel, Swan Commercial hotel
Goulding Alfred, cattle dealer
Goulding Mrs. Mary, coal dealer
Goulding Ralph, carrier & Angel inn
Goulding Thomas, beer retailer
Goulding Walter, baker
Greenman John, saddler
Hanks Henry & Son, tailors
Harris William, farmer
Hill Charles, police sergeant
Hill Henry, baker
Hill Henry, chimney sweeper
Hill Miss Matilda, dressmaker
Hillier Douglas, farmer
Hillier John Goodenough, farmer
Jobbins Henry, mason
Jobbins John, baker
Jobbins William, pig dealer
Jones Thomas, shopkeeper
Kington Moses, hurdle maker
Liddiard John, marine store dealer
Longford William, land measurer
Matthews Richard, butcher
Melsome Robert, farmer
Merchant Edmd. blacksmith & beer rtl
Mills Simeon, boot maker
Neal Edward, farmer & butcher
Neal Edwin, shoe maker

Above: The 'Cliff', c. 1925, where the supposed battle between Canute and Edmund Ironside took place in 1016. John Rattlebone received his wound whilst defending King and Country.

Below: Sherston Magna's old Market Place, c. 1915, now the High Street.

Above: Easton Town, from the Church tower, c. 1915. Note the hay ricks in the Carpenters Arms' field. The large tree also seen in the field, which is now Easton Square, was planted at the same time as the Jubilee tree, and was to be used if the Jubilee tree did not flourish.
Below: Mr Dickenson's shop at the north end of the High Street; c. 1940.

Above: View of the High Street from the Church tower, looking south; c. 1930.

Below: Back Street, c. 1910.

Above: Back Street, c. 1915. Below: The photographer is standing at the junction of Sandpits Lane, looking west towards the village. The photograph must be pre-1904 since the old rectory, which was demolished in 1904 when it became unsafe, is just visible behind and to the left of the Rattlebone (behind small tree).

THE

Parish Magazine

FOR

SHERSTON WITH PINKNEY.

NOVEMBER, 1905.

Price 2d.

TETBURY:

THOMAS HILL, PRINTER, STATIONER, &c., LONG STREET.

Left: Cover of the Parish Magazine, November 1905. Local shops and businesses used the magazine for advertising.

Below: A Demand note and receipt for the Parish Rates, dated 6 January 1924 and addressed to the Co-operative Milling Society. In 1907 Mr Roland Brinkworth, schoolmaster, was the Clerk to the Parish Council and assistant overseer and Collector of Taxes. In 1911 Mr Walter Jobbins took over the former two positions and Mr Brinkworth continued collecting the taxes.

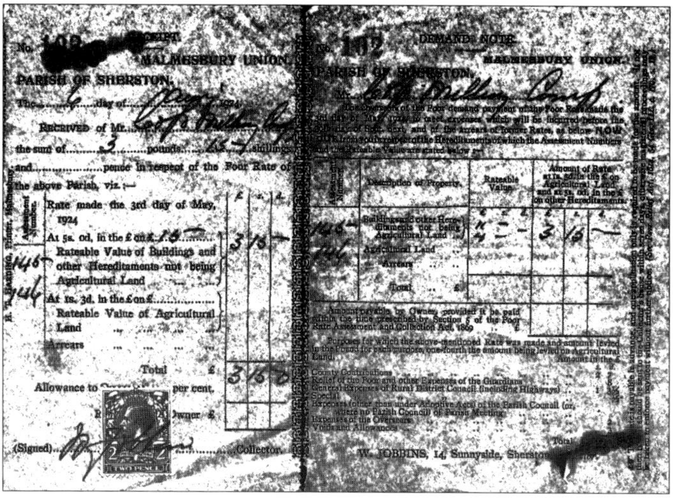

No. RECEIPT.

MALMESBURY UNION.

PARISH OF SHERSTON.

The 6 day of 1924

RECEIVED of Mr.

the sum of 3 pounds shillings

and pence in respect of the Poor Rate of the above Parish, viz.:—

Rate made the 3rd day of May, 1924

At 5s. 0d. in the £ on £ Rateable Value of Buildings and other Hereditaments not being Agricultural Land — 3 15 —

At 1s. 3d. in the £ on £ Rateable Value of Agricultural Land

Arrears

Total £ 3 15 0

Allowance to per cent.

Owner £

(Signed) Collector.

DEMAND NOTE

No.

MALMESBURY UNION.

PARISH OF SHERSTON.

Mr.

Assessment Number	Description of Property	Rateable Value	Amount of Rate at 1s. 3d. in the £ on Agricultural Land and at 5s. 0d. in the £ on other Hereditaments
	Buildings and other Hereditaments not being Agricultural Land		3 15 —
	Agricultural Land		
	Arrears		
	Total £		

Amount payable by Owner, provided it be paid within the time prescribed by Section 5 of the Poor Rate Assessment and Collection Act, 1869 £

Purposes for which the above-mentioned Rate was made and amount levied in the Pound for each purpose, one-fourth the amount being levied on Agricultural Land.

Amount in the £

County Contributions

Relief of the Poor and other Expenses of the Guardians

General Expenses of Rural District Council (including Highways)

Special

Expenses (other than under Adoptive Acts) of the Parish Council (or, where no Parish Council) of Parish Meeting

Expenses of the Overseers

Voids and Allowances

Total

W. JOBBINS, 14, Sunnyside, Sherston

2 The Lord of the Manor

The Anglo Saxons reached Sherston in about the year 577, bringing with them their methods of life, religion, and justice. In their way of life every man was a freeman and a warrior. They dwelt in small communities in which each family would be responsible for the wrongdoings of his family. Differences between villages and families were settled at first by the sword, but later on, were referred to the *Gemot*, or parliament of chief men. It was at a Gemot held by Ethelred at Gloucester in the year 896 that Sherston, or *Scorranstone*, was first mentioned.

The head man, or, as he was known, Ealdorman, attained this position by strength in battle or by descent from some great leader. Later on this position gradually changed to that of lord of the manor. Some of the previous lords of the manor of Sherston were: Baron Robert de Harcourt in 1168, Edward de Bonum in 1333, and Hugh de Despencer in 1340. In more recent times the title has been held by WH Cresswell, CR Estcourt Cresswell, and Mrs Clutterbuck, lady of the manor.

In every manor there were men appointed by the Manor Court, or Court Leet, to supervise the sale of common articles such as bread and ale. Every manor had to have two ale tasters, a constable and bailiff — to weigh the baker's bread every month, searchers and sealers of leather, and one hayward, the officer in charge of fences and enclosures.

In the records, or *Rolls*, of Sherston Manor Court held on the 12th April 1672 before Richard Goodenough, Steward to the Court of Thomas Estcourt Knight, it was reported that the gallows and tumbrel cart had not been erected and repaired as by order of the last Court, and the sum of 3s. 3d. be forfeited. Also that the Constable and Bailiff had not weighed the baker's bread and that Thomas Hobbs laid manure on the highway next to the house of Thomas Palmer, and 'that it is removed before the tenth of May next.'

The Steward would also preside over the paying of fines and market dues as well as the Ale Feast that took place every Whitsun at the Church House. During the Ale Feast the Steward would issue orders for the regulation of trade, see to repairs, and act much like today's Parish Council.

The Steward's officers also herded stray cattle into the Pound where they were kept until all fines were paid. The Sherston Pound still stands near the Sopworth-Knockdown cross-roads.

This ancient system of law and order came to an end with the 1922 Law and Property Act. However, it was in 1936 at a dinner held in the Rattlebone Inn to mark the end of this historic institution, that Mr M Chubb, who had been Steward for over fifty years, made some interesting comments about the Court Leet. He referred to a problem that had been causing concern for many, many years, as to 'who was responsible for the repairs to no-man's land' — the land that ran either side of the main High Street, through the centre of the Parish. He declared that some folk held him responsible for the non repair by the Lord of the Manor; but he put the liability on the County Council, as the Highway Authority, and went on to say that there was not a single Manor in all of England where the Lords of the Manor had ever been called upon to repair the roads. He also threw out a challenge to anyone to say under what Act of Parliament, or custom in any county this was done. He continued that he was unable to say whose liability it was to do the repairs, but bearing in mind that the tenants of houses on either side of the main road must of necessity use this no-man's land to gain access to their dwellings, he was of the opinion that the onus was on the County Council.

In 1950 this same argument was still going on, and at the Parish Council meeting on the 25 September, the committee was told that the County Council would carry out temporary repairs to the margins either side of the High Street.

Eventually, in about 1953, after the new sewage pipes had been laid, the County Council resurfaced the main High Street and no-man's land, but unfortunately at the cost of the annual Trinity Monday Fair. The organisers were then forced to use the Recreation Ground to put up their rides and shows.

Once Lord of the Manor, M.S. Estcourt Cresswell Esq., now lies in Sherston's churchyard.

3 Pinkney Park

Of all the ghost stories that have been told over the years, the one that most people of Sherston know best relates to the *Blood stained door of Pinkney Park*.

Pinkney, or Sherston Parva, is a small hamlet about one mile outside Sherston. The Park belonged to the Estcourt family until 1704 when Thomas Estcourt died. The estate then passed, along the female line of the family, to Elizabeth Estcourt. Elizabeth married Richard Cresswell who was known as *Black Dick* because of his dark and menacing appearance.

Richard and Elizabeth had a son, Thomas Estcourt Cresswell, who, it appears, was a thoroughly bad lot! In the Press of 1747 the story of his triple bigamy became known. The story continues that one of the servant girls at the house knew a little too much about Thomas for her own good, and that he is supposed to have murdered her. With his hands covered in her blood, he left a hand print on the door.

Some time after the second World War, the house, having fallen into decay, was sold, with the interior wood panelling being shipped out to South Africa. The door with the stain was removed and taken to Mr Tom Neal's workshop where several attempts were made to remove the stains. They even resorted to using a blow torch. All to no avail – nothing could remove the mark.

The old house has long since gone, and a new one is built on to the old stable block.

Lt Col Wyatt William Turnor, standing in the entrance to Pinkney Park, c. 1930.

Above: The rose walk in front of the ballroom at Pinkney Park House, c. 1930.

Below: Pinkney Park House.

4 The fourteenth century Village Cross

Up until 1835 Sherston was a Borough with a municipal corporation of some kind, until it was deprived of its charter. In early documents relating to old houses in Sherston during the 15th century, these houses were referred to as *Burgages*, which meant houses in a Borough. The charter, creating Sherston a Borough, was in John Rattlebone's chest in the year 1656. The town also had its own Mayor and Corporation until 1835.

Three market crosses marked the boundary of the Borough. It is understood that the crosses were sited at the top of Noble Street, one at Forlorn, and one in the High Street, next to the building now known as The Tolsey. All the crosses were believed to have been standing until 1814. However, the base of only one of them remains. This exceedingly rare relic today stands in the garden of the present vicarage. The base is in a reasonable condition and is a reminder of Sherston's past importance.

The Parish Council once considered moving the base to a more suitable site, and adding a cross to provide a War Memorial.

The base of the remaining village cross, as it stands today. Though badly eroded, traces of the stonemason's artistry are still detectable.

CLUBS AND ORGANISATIONS

1 Sherston Cricket Club

The menfolk of Sherston have enjoyed playing the game of cricket as far back as the fifteenth century, when it was then known as 'Stoolball'. Using an upturned milking stool as the wicket, the defender would strike at the opponent's ball which was made from leather stuffed with reed. His 'staffe', or bat, was made usually from withy, and would be approximately forty-two inches in length. A point would be scored each time the defender hit the ball.

In 1634 the Archbishop of Canterbury stated *many games and pastimes occupy people, when they ought to be at church, both on Sundays and Holydays*, and in particular, mentioned the people of Sherston, and the playing of Stoolball.

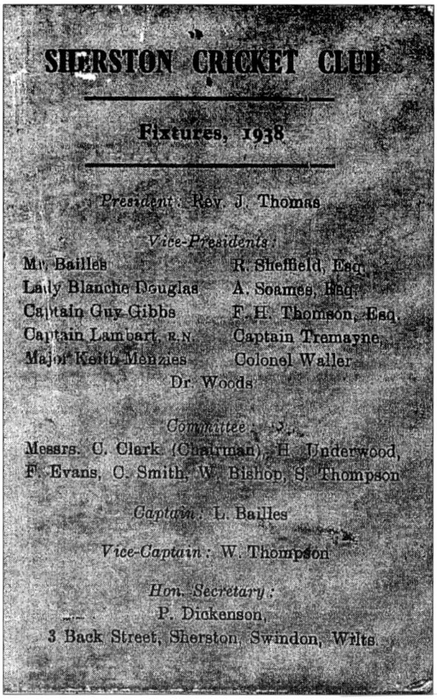

SHERSTON CRICKET CLUB

Fixtures, 1938

President: Rev. J. Thomas

Vice-Presidents:

Mr. Bailles	R. Sheffield, Esq.
Lady Blanche Douglas	A. Soames, Esq.
Captain Guy Gibbs	F. H. Thomson, Esq.
Captain Lambart, R.N.	Captain Tremayne
Major Keith Menzies	Colonel Waller

Dr. Woods

Committee:

Messrs. C. Clark (Chairman), H. Underwood, F. Evans, C. Smith, W. Bishop, S. Thompson

Captain: L. Bailles

Vice-Captain: W. Thompson

Hon. Secretary:
P. Dickenson,
3 Back Street, Sherston, Swindon, Wilts.

In the 1930s, in the grounds of Pinkney Park, the village had their cricket pitch. A perfect location to spend a warm Sunday afternoon in the shade of the trees, watching an exciting game of cricket. Billy Thompson, who was vice-captain in 1938, provided his Chrysler motor van to convey the teas, which had been prepared by the wives of the team members and were served in the large tea tent.

After many years of being without a permanent pitch, the village cricket team are again playing at Pinkney Park.

Above: Members of Sherston cricket team in 1938.
Front row (l-r): Arthur Dickenson, Tommy Tremlin, Tom Neal, Sam Thompson, Bill Thompson, Mackie Bishop, (on the ground) David Thompson. Back row (l-r): Dennis Ritchings, Peter Dickenson, Gilbert Rickards, Arthur Berry, Sandy Pritchard, Cecil Clarke, Charlie Smith, Bert Cousins.
Below: Relaxing in the tea tent at Pinkney Park in 1938. Foreground (l-r): Sandy Pritchard, Cecil Clarke, Peter Dickenson, Sam Thompson, Bill Thompson.

2 Sherston Town Football Club

Sherston people have always been proud of their football teams, but in 1920 their support was needed more than ever when one of the players was accused of unsportsmanlike, cowardly conduct. The incident happened during one of the two Yuletide matches, traditionally played between Sherston and Malmesbury. As reported in the local paper, the encounters between these two teams have never been of the 'parlour' type of football, and on this occasion they certainly were not.

The first of the two matches was played at Sherston and resulted in a home win of 4-1; but the second match was taking a different course, and at half time, Malmesbury was winning by two goals to Sherston's one. Sherston Club, who had taken a contingent of supporters, obviously did not relish defeat, and with the Malmesbury Club and supporters trying their utmost to maintain order and to calm the ruffled Sherstonians, things were not looking too good. The referee, Mr Parrott, was absolutely defied, and probably because he feared a riot, did not exercise his full powers.

With only three minutes left to play, Phil Sharpe, Malmesbury's centre forward, narrowly missed another goal. He was standing easily, when suddenly and without warning, a Sherston player approached him and dealt a staggering blow to the face. First aid was sought from Doctor Pitts, but it was not until the next day that it was found that Sharpe's jaw had been broken and that he was suffering from concussion.

Further action was taken against the Sherston player, who then received a £5 fine and was banned from playing. The player, who does feature in one of the football club photographs, shall remain nameless — he was in fact a close relation of the injured Sharpe!

Sherston Town Football teams have always played in red and white, and in 1939 the sum of £5.6s.8d. was paid to Gyles Bros Ltd, Complete Sports Outfitters, for a dozen football shirts of the best twill, and two Crown T footballs.

Rent for the Carpenter's Arms field cost £5 and was paid to Mr Purnell, on the assurance that any damage done to the walls would be repaired by the Club.

For many years Mr Frank Knapp, well-known publican of the

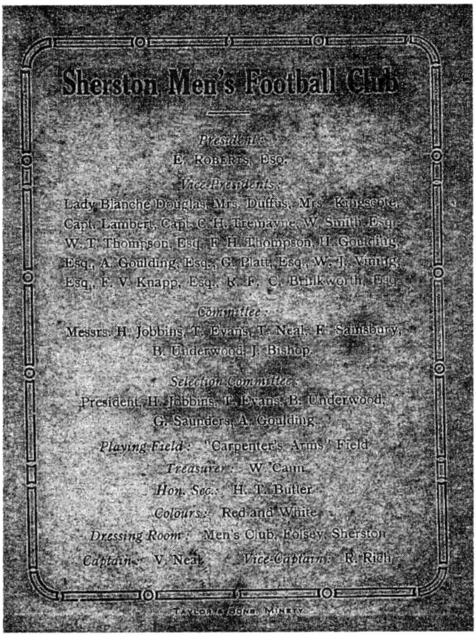

Sherston Men's Football Club

President:
E. Roberts, Esq.

Vice-Presidents:
Lady Blanche Douglas, Mrs. Duffus, Mrs. Kingscote, Capt. Lambert, Capt. C. H. Tremayne, W. Smith, Esq., W. T. Thompson, Esq., F. H. Thompson, H. Goulding, Esq., A. Goulding, Esq., G. Platt, Esq., W. J. Vining, Esq., F. V. Knapp, Esq., R. F. C. Brinkworth, Esq.

Committee:
Messrs. H. Jobbins, T. Evans, T. Neal, F. Sainsbury, B. Underwood, J. Bishop.

Selection Committee:
President, H. Jobbins, T. Evans, B. Underwood, G. Saunders, A. Goulding.

Playing Field: "Carpenter's Arms" Field
Treasurer: W. Cann
Hon. Sec.: H. T. Butler
Colours: Red and White
Dressing Room: Men's Club, Folsey, Sherston
Captain: V. Neal *Vice-Captain:* R. Rich

Taylor & Sons, Minety

Rattlebone Inn, and a County Councillor, played for the Sherston team, and is fondly remembered for one particular home game in which he played. The game was going well, when suddenly Knappie fell to the ground apparently in agony, clutching his legs and screaming to Billy Thompson, "Quick, Bill! I've broke both me legs". A hushed silence fell over the spectators. Then up jumped Knappie and sprinted across the pitch!

Left: Fixtures list, 1939-40.

Below: An invoice, dated 5 August 1939, from Gyles Bros, Complete Sports Outfitters, of Bristol for football clothing and equipment.

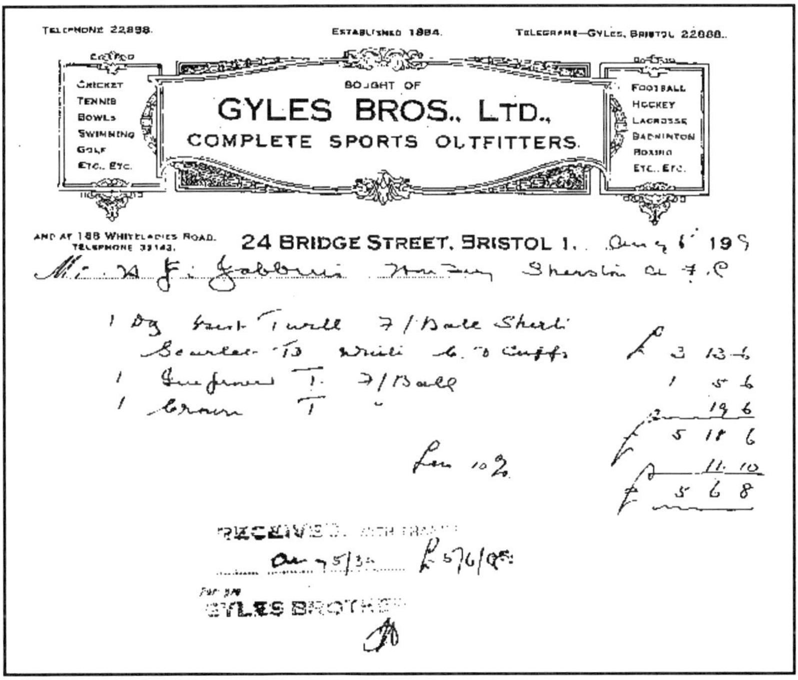

Telephone 22898. Established 1884. Telegrams—Gyles, Bristol 22888.

Cricket
Tennis
Bowls
Swimming
Golf
Etc., Etc.

Bought of
GYLES BROS., LTD.,
COMPLETE SPORTS OUTFITTERS.

Football
Hockey
Lacrosse
Badminton
Boxing
Etc., Etc.

And at 188 Whiteladies Road. Telephone 33143.
24 BRIDGE STREET, BRISTOL 1. Aug 5 1939

Received with thanks
For the
Gyles Brothers

Above: Members of Sherston Athletic Football Club 1913-14
Front (l-r): R Neal, V Jobbins, Arthur (Slen) Neal, Jimmy (Salmon) Evans, Alf Miles. Middle: P Stickler, V Saunders, W Punter, Walt Sherwood, Fred Watts (Easton Grey). Back: Fred Neal (Secretary), A Dicks, F Stickler, Harold Mills, W Lighthowler, G Neal, A Jobbins (Treasurer), Sidney Dickenson (Referee).
It was a member of this team that caused a near riot during the game played against the Malmesbury football team in the annual Yuletide match in 1920.

Below: Sherston Cup football team 1924-5.
Front (l-r): Fred Evans, ?, Billy Thompson, ?, Middle: ?, Cecil Clarke, Frank Knapp, Rev Page, Walt Sherwood, M. Wilcox, ?. Back: George Evans, ?, Bert Underwood, Harold Mills, A Jobbins, 'Bloater' Evans, Mr Stephens, Mr Saunders, ?.

Above: Members of Sherston football team 1929-30
Back(l-r): Mr Saunders, Omar Neal, Fred Sainsbury, Tom Thompson, Mr Stevens, Mr Judkins. Middle: Jack Sheppard, Kilip Palmer, Tom Neal, Rev Cecil Page, Fred Evans, Walter Bishop, Stan Lacey. Front: Wally Camm, Harry Holloway, Jack Bishop, Jack Thompson.

Below: 1933-34
Back (l-r): ?, Frank Knapp, Vernon Neal, ?, Omar Neal, Bill Cousins, Fred Watts.
Middle: Tom Neal, Wally Camm, Tom Thompson, ?.
Front: Sam Thompson, Billy Thompson, Benny Neal, Abbie Berry, Jack Thompson.

3 Sherston Men's Club

During the Depression following the First World War, a not uncommon sight would be groups of men standing by the Jubilee tree. They were all in the same situation of having families to support with little prospect of finding employment, many of them having cycled to Malmesbury to the Labour Exchange in search of work, but for most of them it would be a wasted journey. It was then decided to provide a place for these men to meet and relax. And so, in February 1920, Sherston Men's Club was started at the British School rooms.

The Reverends Walter Page and Walter Povey were joint Presidents. At one of the first meetings, Alderman Evans, Mayor of Swindon, visited the Club. He expressed how glad he was to be invited, as he had lived in Sherston for many years, and he also kindly offered to supply the materials to decorate the rooms. At the end of the meeting Mr George Ford entertained with popular ditties of the day. Miss Evans played a piano solo, and the Reverend Page, who was a very talented singer and composer, sang a solo.

The members of the Club were able to meet and play a game of darts or billiards. There were also climbing ropes suspended from the ceiling beams and dumbbells with which to exercise.

In 1939 the clubhouse was commandeered for National Service, and the dilemma of where to hold their meetings caused major problems for the members. A meeting was called on Monday 20 November to discuss the options open to them. Mr Harold Jobbins took the Chair and stated that alternative accommodation had been sought, but could not be found. It was then suggested that they attempt to raise the money needed to build a clubhouse of their own. It was estimated that this would cost £80; it was suggested members might make a donation of either £1, 10/-, or 5/- to help finance the project. Eventually, however, this was not needed as Mr Wilson, the coal merchant who had his premises in the High Street, kindly offered the use of a hut at the back of his yard.

The original Men's Club membership totalled about sixty men with ages ranging from sixteen to sixty years' old; in 1939 the numbers had dropped considerably due to the outbreak of war.

Nevertheless, the balance sheet showed a healthy profit. Money raised for the Club was through subscriptions, dances, whist drives, billiard games, concerts, and even the sale of chalk. Expenses included the installation of electric light in the club house, coke and wood for heating, engraving cups, and dart league dinners.

As the war continued, the Club became smaller and smaller, and eventually it was decided to unite the Men's Club with the Sherston Football Club. This club continued to support the village football team for many years. They held their meetings in the Tolsey, which by then belonged to the Royal British Legion.

The original Congregational Men's Club, taken in the chapel grounds next to the Manse, c. 1919.
Front (l-r): Tommy Watkins, ?, Charlie Sherwood, ?, ?, Ken Dickenson, Percy Harris.
2nd. row: R Lacey, ?, Chris Ball, Colin Curtis, Arthur Long, Rev. Daniels, Tom Sherwood, ?, ?, ?, Bacca Sainsbury.
3rd. row: ? Neal, Fred (Lolum) Neal, ?, ?, ?, ?, Tom Palmer, Walter Rice, Chookie Palmer.
Back: Roy Sainsbury, ? Cooper, Reg Evans, Gilbert Neal, Billy Thompson, Bill Evans, ?, ? Stephens, ?, ?.

Above: A group of men standing outside the Rattlebone Inn, 1920. It was at this time that the Men's Club was started.
Below: A Sherston Men's Club card, 1939-42.

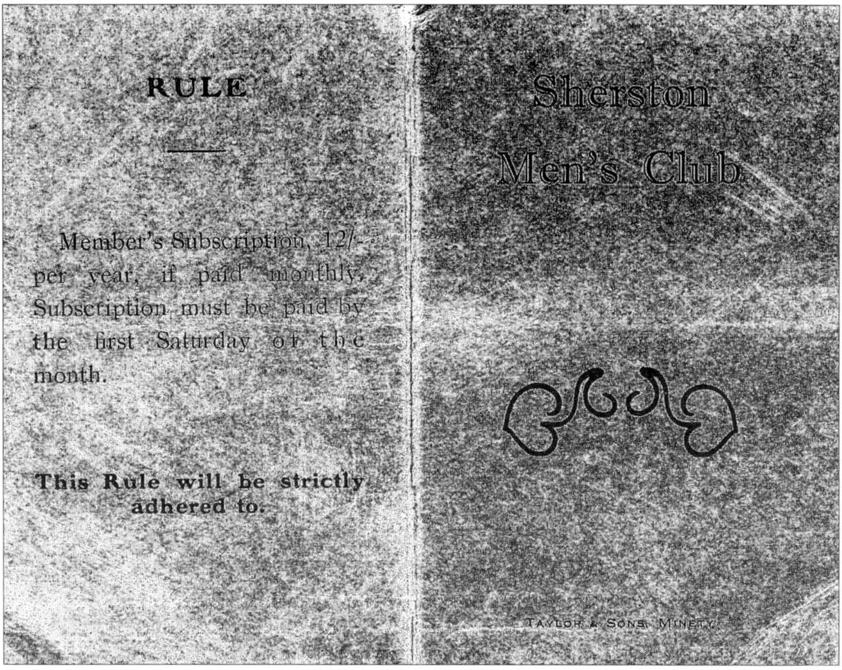

RULE

Member's Subscription, 12/- per year, if paid monthly. Subscription must be paid by the first Saturday of the month.

This Rule will be strictly adhered to.

Sherston Men's Club

TAYLOR & SONS, MINETY.

4 The Workers' Union

The Sherston branch of the Workers' Union began in about 1918. The aim of the Union was to offer association for all — from the carter, ploughman, and cowman, to the worker in wood and iron — no craft was excluded. Not only did it give encouragement to the rural farm workers to fight for fair wages, but also assistance to those members on strike. To help raise funds various schemes were promoted by the members.

One such endeavour was a fete and carnival, with the proceeds being divided between the Union, Malmesbury Hospital, and the Bristol Royal Infirmary. Music on the day was provided by the Sherston Town Band, under the leadership of Ernest Clark. Events staged at the fete included local sprinters, long-distance runners, football, a tug-of-war, pillow fights, and bowling for a pig.

Ernie Rule won first prize for the best decorated four-wheeled vehicle, with Reg Clarke winning the best two-wheeled vehicle. The one-mile flat race was won by Billy Thompson, with H Vickery taking second prize, and Harold Mills third. Billy Thompson was also the winner of the pillow fight. The half-mile flat race was won by Inkerman (Inky) Rice, with Fred Wiltshire coming a close second.

It was not all work for the Union members, as various trips and outings were arranged. One of these outings took place for the Sherston men in July 1920. Eighty-one members of the Union enjoyed a fine outing to Clevedon.

Being favoured with glorious weather, three charabancs conveyed the party, and the journey, in these comfortable vehicles, was most pleasantly made. The journey began at 7.45am and went by way of Stroud, Gloucester, and Bristol, eventually reaching Clevedon at 4.00pm! An hour and a half's stay allowed the trippers the opportunity to indulge themselves in various ways, with the return journey from the seaside town departing at 6.30pm. A jolly run home was undertaken, Sherston being reached late at night without the slightest mishap having occurred.

Above: The Workers' Union outing to Weymouth, c. 1930. Participants assembled in their transport, the Morning Star Greyhound coach.
Jack (Clubby) Liddiard is second from left in the back row, smoking a cigarette; in front of him is Mr Horton; Fred (lolum) Neal is third from the right; fourth from the right, Duncan Neale; third from right, Wilf (Wacker) Neal, with Cecil Berry leaning next to him. Jack Bishop is the young lad sat on the hood at the back.

Tom Goulding (left) and Ernie Rule in front of their decorated vehicle at the Fete and Carnival in 1922.

5 Toc H

Tubby Clayton was the founder of the Toc H movement in France during the First World War. His aim was to provide care and comfort for soldiers wounded in battle. After the War, the movement continued with meetings being held in villages all around the country.

In Sherston these meetings took place at Johnny Minett's home in a room above his shop. After the Second World War the Toc H was revived again, and now the men met in the small room at the British School rooms.

The meetings began with the lighting of the Toc H oil lamp. Some of the members who attended included Peter Dickenson, Joe Minett, Gordon Sainsbury, Tom Cambourne, William Berry, Charlie West, Ray Smith, Dennis Ritchings, Reg Wilcox, and Charles Dyson. The Sherston branch was proud of their group and even attended an assembly at the Albert Hall in London, when the village banner was carried.

6 Sherston Scouts and Wolf Cubs

The Scouts and Wolf Cub movement began in Sherston about 1929. The first meetings were held in a barn at the Tan House on Tanners Hill.

In December 1931 the Troop enjoyed a very jolly Christmas party, with cakes and sandwiches being provided by Mrs Minett, Mrs Gough and others.

The Rev W Cecil Page, who had been involved with the troop since it began, and had donated such gifts as wood working tools, cricket pads, and so on, was given a rousing cheer. Prizes were handed out to the best Cub who was Joe Minett, and the prize for the best Scout went to C Evans. After camp fire songs and carols, the meeting broke up.

Earlier in the month, the cubs and Scouts had sung carols around the village. They raised over £1 which went into the fund to build a permanent Scouts' Headquarters.

Scouts and Cubs at Budleigh Salterton, Devon in August 1954 Top row (l-r): Geoff Wicks, John Walsh, David Poole, Mrs D Dyson, Mr AG Dyson (Skipper), Alan Evans, Ken Wilcox, Graham Wilcox. Middle row (l-r): John Evans, David Graves, Philip Bishop, David Punter, Derek Bishop, Tony Neal, Terry Sly, Michael Poole, John Osbourne, Derek James. Front: Michael Anthony, John Pritchard, Trevor Sly.

In April 1931 the Cubs and Scouts had a stall at the Church Fete, where they sold artefacts in wood and iron that they had made, as well as nearly-new gramophone records. The proceeds from the sale would go towards purchasing a tent and cricket materials.

The Girl Guides and Brownies started in the village a few years later, and they too were eager fund-raisers. A concert was held at the Rifle Range in December 1936. Mrs West as Captain arranged the concert with the help of Miss Platt (Brown Owl). The sum raised on the night for the Guides' fund was £6.17.11d.

Eventually, in April 1962, the official opening ceremony for the newly built Scouts' and Guides' Headquarters took place at Sandpits Lane. This was used for many years until the housing estate at Manor Close was built. The Headquarters were then rebuilt on the Recreation Field.

Opening Day, 28 April 1962 (l-r): AG Dyson (Skipper), JH Marty, D McCombs, SMC Thayr (County Commander), F Sheldon, who performed the opening ceremony.

The first Sherston Scout and Guide HQ, Sandpits Lane, 1962.

The first Sherston Guides and Brownies, April 1962.

7 The Sherston Good Templars

The Good Templars were all members of the Temperance movement. In Sherston the founder members included Brothers T Taylor, Clement Palser (shopkeeper), and Henry Hanks (tailor).

Mr Hanks, who was born in Sherston in 1819, had been an abstainer from intoxicating liquor since 1864.

The Temperance meetings were held in the British School rooms in Back Street. On 27 April 1872 they enjoyed a meeting which included recitations and choir singing and finished up with 'a nice cup of tea'.

8 'C' Company, The 2nd Battalion: Wiltshire Home Guard

'Not so quiet on the Home Front!'

The broadcast appeal which called the Local Defence Volunteers into being was delivered by Mr Anthony Eden on the evening of 14 May 1940. In his appeal he recorded: "I want to speak to you tonight about the form of warfare that the Germans have been using, mainly the dropping of troops by parachute behind the main defence lines". He went on to ask for large numbers of men between the ages of 15 to 65 to come forward now and offer their services, and explained "You will not be paid but you will receive a uniform, and you will be armed".

When the Sherston volunteers received their uniforms they were also given armbands on which were emblazoned the initials LDV — humorously interpreted as standing for *Look, Duck and Vanish!*

The men were all very proud of their smart new uniforms. However, very few of them had weapons, except for the odd shotgun or pike handle. On one occasion the platoon was on guard duty at the Fosse railway line. Lt Frank Knapp was in command, and said to one of the men:

"Here, Jack, I hope you ain't got nought up the spout of that rifle."

"No, course I ain't" came the reply.

With that he pulled the trigger and a loud explosion shattered the silence; thankfully nobody was in the line of fire.

By 1940 the LDV became the Home Guard, and over 15,000 local men had joined Wiltshire platoons. The area covered by the Sherston platoon included the villages of Sherston, Luckington, Alderton, Sopworth, and Easton Grey. Captain E Green MC was Commander, with Lt FV Knapp, 2nd Lt WJ Vining, 2nd Lt W Thompson, Lt RW Horsham, 2nd Lt R Padfield, Lt AG Jolliffe, 2nd Lt WGS Parson as platoon Commanders, with a strength of 138 men.

In October 1942 there was a tragedy in the Platoon when Private William Dando was accidentally killed during manoeuvres. Private Dando is buried in a war grave in Sherston churchyard.

Private George Strong VC is also buried in the churchyard. He was awarded the VC in September 1855 for an act of gallantry in the trenches at Sebastopol.

The villagers were very proud of their Home Guard and when the end of the war was nearing and the order came for it to be disbanded, the village held a farewell dinner at the Rifle Range. It was held on 9 December 1944 at 7.00pm. The menu included sausages and mashed potato, apple dumplings and custard, and beer and minerals with which to drink a toast to the men of the Sherston Home Guard.

27 December 1941: Arthur Palmer in uniform outside the Old Pharmacy in the High Street. The windows have been taped to prevent the glass shattering in the event of bombs being dropped.

Above:"C" Company 2nd Battalion, Sherston's Home Guard, photographed in the Recreation Field in 1940.
Front row (seated on ground, l-r): Omar Dickenson, Chris Berry, Arthur Long, Wilf Parker, George Pickford, Ronald Smart, Melvin Bishop, Len Butler, Fred Bishop, Harold Dash, Sonny Dickenson.
2nd row (seated): Bill Dickenson, Norman Richards, Harold Jobbins, Bill Thompson, Frank Knapp, Captain Green, Jack Vining, Harold Mills, Harry Pomeroy, ?, Wilf Neal.
3rd row (behind seated): John Thompson, Frank Pickett, Cyril Harris, Jack Dolman, Harry Goble, Charles Sherwood, ?, Percy Wilkins, Tom Evans, Bill Hadland, ?, Jack Lacey, Jack Long, Stan Lacey.
4th row: Jack Palmer, Cecil Stephens, Omar Neal, Charles Giles, ?, Cecil Clarke, Stan Hannam, ?, Bill Evans.
Back row (l-r): Herbert Evans, John Howarth, Dick James, Walter Rice, Reg Rice, ?, Herbert Neal, Jack Browning, Bert Berry.

Opposite: The cover of a menu card for A Farewell Dinner of "C" Company 2nd Battalion, Wiltshire Home Guard.

"C" Company

2nd Battalion - Wilts Home Guard

A Farewell Dinner

will be given in

THE RIFLE RANGE, SHERSTON

on

Saturday, Dec. 9th, 1944

at 7-0 p.m.

EDUCATION

1 The National School

An old barn, belonging to the Rectory that stood behind the Rattlebone Inn, was demolished in 1845 to make way for the village school. The Rectory itself, thought to have been built in the thirteenth century, was finally pulled down in 1904, after becoming unsafe. Before this it had been used as the village Post Office.

The school was of a mixed Elementary to hold 270 children. From 1883 George Dear was the Master, with Roland Brinkworth as assistant. In the September of 1910 Mr Dear made this last entry in the school Log Book: "A notice from the Board of Education arrived today, and stated that my Certificate expires on this day. This closes my school career. I complete today the 27th year of work in this school. I can only say goodbye to a much loved work, and subscribe myself George Dear". The next entry, made on 16 September 1910, was as follows:

"I commence my duties as Headmaster this morning after being assistant here since 1898. There are 128 children present today. Signed R. Brinkworth".

Another entry found regularly in the Log Book would be from Mr Seager, the Truant Officer, who would look over the Register and check that the children were attending school regularly, *and if not, why not?*

Sister Mary Anne Lewis would make regular visits to the school to check the children for verminous hair! And to dish out cod liver oil to the children. Also Doctor Fletcher would often be called in to order the school to be closed at any sign of an epidemic, usually of the influenza or impetigo. On one occasion the school was closed for three weeks due to an outbreak of influenza, which, in those days, could often prove to be fatal.

Mr Dear, Mr Brinkworth, and, later, Mr Warren were all very

keen on the idea that the boys should learn how to grow vegetables, and so in the field at the back of the school, the boys all kept allotments. The boys spent hours working the soil, and if any were caught misbehaving in class, and not paying attention to their lessons, they were sent out to 'trench' the gardens. The money raised by the sale of vegetables, and the honey that was also produced from bee hives in the gardens, was then spent on the purchase of seeds and new gardening tools. Whilst the boys were gardening, the girls would be learning to knit and sew, and even how to cook and clean!

In 1925 the school was visited by the County Domestic Cookery and Laundry class, under the instruction of Miss Brewerton. The class was held in the Rifle Range, with the Council providing a coal-fired stove and all the equipment that was needed. And so, as soon as assembly had ended and the Register completed, the girls went over to the Rifle Range and began their lessons. In the mornings they learnt how to bake cakes and pies, and to roast and fry. In the afternoon it was the laundry and cleaning class.

The course lasted for two weeks, and then would move on to other schools in the County. The girls that attended were eleven years' old, and would have another opportunity when they were aged thirteen. As many of these girls would later go into domestic service, these classes were very beneficial.

The normal school day began at 9.00am with the Register being called, followed by Assembly, a short bible reading, hymns, prayers, and a talk from Mr Brinkworth. Then the day's lessons began — sums, reading, writing, and spelling, arts and crafts, and singing.

At the age of eleven the children from the surrounding villages would attend Sherston School, using bicycles provided by the Council. Most of them would bring sandwiches for their lunch, or go to Mr 'Rattle' Jobbins across the road and buy a bag of chips from his Fish & Chip shop.

A child's education at Sherston School would be complete at his, or her, fourteenth birthday. Unless they had passed the entrance exam to the Grammar School at Malmesbury, they would have to begin their working life, most of them leaving with fond memories of their time at Sherston School.

Above: Sherston National School, 1910. Mr Dear, the Headmaster, is standing on the left, and Mr Roland Brinkworth, Deputy Head, on the right.

Above: 1926-27: Front row (l-r): Jimmy Butler, Gilbert Rickard, Freddie Wallace, ?, ?.
2nd row: Billy Saunders, Ted Scarrott, George Smith,?, Billy Hadland, Mary Stickler, Louie Hadland, Muriel Wilcox, Phyllis Evans.
3rd row: Sonny Dickenson, Stanley Hunt, Donald Stephens, Wilson Thompson, Reg Clarke, Marnie Strong, Vera Broad, Betty Saunders, Dolly Warner.
Back: Melvyn Bishop,? Whybrow,? Thompson, Thirza Peters, Rose Clarke, Gladys Cooper, Dolly Grant.

Opposite below: The boys' gardening class, c. 1910. Several tons of stones were unearthed when the boys began work on clearing the gardens. The stones probably came from the old rectory that once stood on the site. Local historians hoped to find subterranean passages, running from the Cliff to the church, but none were ever found. The stones were utilised in the gardens' paths and borders.

Above: 1927-8
Front (l-r): Gladys Hadland, Ivy Hadland, Betty Wallace, Kathlyn Evans, Elsie Rickards.
2nd row: Gilbert Rickards, Louie Hadland, Mabel Evans, Phyllis Evans.
3rd row: Headmaster: Mr Roland Brinkworth, Jimmy Butler, Ted Scarrott, George Smith, Arthur Law, ? Whybrow, Bill Hadland, Richard Stevens, Fred Wallace.
Back: Donald Stephens, ? Thompson, ? Thompson, Cyril Evans, ? Whybrow, ? Thompson, Bertie Neal.

Opposite below: 1930: Front (l-r): Gertie Wilcox, Vera Underwood, Kathleen Evans, Doris Dickenson, Miss Mortimer (teacher), Daisy Thompson, Hilda Osborne, Bertha Kington, Mary Nurdin.
2nd row: Joan Pritchard, Margaret Sherwood, Peggy Purnell, Ivy Hadland, Evelyn Neal, Muriel Neal, Jean Isherwood, Bubbles Ball, Margaret Mackelon.
3rd row: Dorothy Milsom, Irene Andrews, Kitty Curtis, Doris Hill, Kathleen Bishop, Joan Howard, Vera Curtis, Winnie Hill, Betty Wallace.
Back row: Joan Andrews, Doris Skull, Vera Butler, Eva Isaacs.

Above: 1929-30
Front row (l-r): Donald Neal, Lionel Glass, Fred (Flyer) Rice, ?, ?, Joan Pritchard, Dorcas Butler, Rose Gregory, Hannah Gregory, ?, Leonard Rice, Topsy Hadland, Geoffrey Clarke.
2nd row: ?, Harry Butler, Bubbles Ball, George Clifford, Daisy Thompson, Richard Aggett, Vivien Carter, ?, Arthur Dickenson, Leonard Butler, Reg Outlaw, Betty Palmer.
Back row: Billy Carter, Gordon Sainsbury, ?, Doris Dickenson, Fred Watts, Iris Glass, Joe Minett, Gordon Thompson, Molly Jobbins, ?, ?, ?.

Above: 1929:
Front (l-r): Betty Palmer, Betty Warner, Jean Hardcastle (teacher), Rose Saunders, Pat Smith.
2nd: Topsy Hadland, Margaret Dickenson, Grace Langdown, Bubbles Ball, Betty Dickenson, Madge Judkins, Betty Horton, Gloria Hale.
3rd: Eric Hadland, Fred Smith, Freddie Rice, Dennis Goulding, Herbie Long, ?, Ivor Jobbins.
Back: Fred Isherwood, Len Butler, Richard Aggett, ?, Henry Hill, George Clifford, Fred Sherwood, ?.

The School's Cookery and Laundry Class, c. 1926, held in the Rifle Range.
Front row (l-r): Marnie Strong, Rose Clarke, Dorothy Smith, Thirza Peters, Gladys Cooper.
Back row: Dolly Grant, Dorothy Butler, Phyllis Holbrow, Betty Saunders, Miss Girling (teacher), Dolly Scarrott, Edie Cawson.

2 The British School Room, Back Street

In 1844 the British School Room was opened in Back Street. The majority of the pupils that attended were from families that were in business. A fee of tuppence per week was charged, which would have been far beyond the means of the average family.

My great grandmother, Amy Sainsbury, taught at the school, and as some of the pupils were as young as three years' old, it was not unusual for them to fall asleep in her arms.

Mr Seldon was the Headmaster until 1902. He was also the organist at the Congregational Chapel.

Great Uncle Arthur (Slen) Neale was the caretaker at the School room. One of the jobs he attended to was adding the water to the carbide bottles, which produced the gas needed to light the gas lamps.

In the late 1950s the School Room was used as a dining room for the Primary School. Every lunch time the 'dinner' ladies would lead the children across the main road and up Swan Barton, where their lunch was waiting. The dinners were cooked at Malmesbury School, and then sent out to the surrounding villages in the dinner van.

Now the School Room is used for private functions and the Senior Citizens' meetings.

Mr Seldon, Headmaster at the British School Room until 1902.

Above: Sherston British School 1881
Mr William J Sheldon, Headmaster, is on the right, and Mr Williams, Assistant Teacher, on the left.

Below: Sherston British School 1881
Small boys' and girls' class; Eva Weaver, Assistant Teacher, is on the left.

Above: Mrs Sarah Seldon (née Berry) and the class of girls, c 1891.
Below: Amy and Harry Sainsbury, my paternal great grandparents; this photograph was taken in the garden of their home in Back Street in about 1930.

Amy's first husband, Arthur Neale, had died in his twenties, leaving Amy with a young baby. It was at this time that she helped teach at the School rooms opposite her home.

Harry came to Sherston from Charfield in about 1890. His family were all silk weavers, and he came to work at the silk mills as works' manager. He lodged at Amy's house through the week, returning home at the weekend.

They eventually married in 1892 and then had a son, Vernon, my grandfather. Amy and Harry died within a year of each other in 1936 and 1937.

Sherston Senior Club outside the British School rooms 1968-9.
Seated (l-r): Mrs Dyer, Mrs Amos, Mrs G Neal, Mrs R Berry, Mrs Moyles, Mrs T Neal, Mrs W Dickenson, Mrs Gregory, Mrs Rice, Mrs Barber, Mrs N Bird, Mrs W Outlaw, Mrs W Berry (née Sainsbury), Mr W Berry.
Standing: Mrs Jolliffe, Mrs Harvey, Mr Jolliffe, ?, Miss Clark, ?, Mrs Ward, ?, Mrs Wilcox, ?, Mrs Evans, Mrs Blanchard, Rev Parsons, Mrs Andrews, Mrs Scrivens, ?, Mr Saunders, Mr Ray Smith, ?, ?, Rev Grant, ?, Mrs Widow Evans, Albert (Drip) Evans, Mr Vining, Mr Marshall, Mrs Rice, Mrs Bird, Mrs A Berry, Mrs Vining, Mrs Platt, Mrs C Clarke.

3 The Children's Guild

In 1905 there were approximately 118 children attending the Children's Guild. The Guild had been introduced to provide a place for the youngsters of the village to learn basic crafts and skills.

For the girls these crafts included sewing, doll-dressing, netting, macramé, and scrap book making. The boys learnt chair caning, fretwork, and carpentry. Even for the infants there was kindergarten and knitting.

The items produced by these children were then sold at fetes and sales to provide the funds for the materials.

SHERSTON CHILDREN'S GUILD.

BALANCE SHEET, JAN.-MAY, 1905.

	£	s.	d.
By Balance in hand	0	19	8½
,, Children's payments ...	1	17	6½
,, Chairs caned	0	7	0
,, Sale of two window boxes	0	5	0
,, Sale of sewing articles . .	0	4	0½
,, Sale of netted bag ...	0	0	3
,, Balance due to treasurer	0	9	5½
	£4	3	0

	£	s.	d.
To Mrs. Hewetson, cleaning, &c.	0	8	0
,, materials for sewing ...	0	6	9
,, ,, ,, fretwork ...	0	5	6
,, ,, ,, carpentering	0	14	9
,, ,, ,, crochet ...	0	2	6½
,, ,, ,, netting ...	0	1	9
,, ,, ,, scrapbooks	0	0	4
,, oil for lamps	0	12	9
,, share of fuel & wear & tear	0	10	0
,, bread and cake for tea on April 10th	1	0	7½
	£4	3	0

WORSHIP

1 The Congregational Chapel

In 1825 a farmer Cook purchased a barn in Back Street and had it transformed into the Congregational Chapel.

For well over twenty-two years the Reverend Walter Povey, a highly respected and admired man, was Minister. After his death, he was laid to rest in his beloved Chapel's burial ground.

The organ in the Chapel was purchased in 1923. Mrs Minett was the organist. She would often call upon children in the congregation to take turns to pump the bellows at the side of the organ, to produce the music. If it happened to be Leslie Neal's turn, he was never too sure of the duration of some of the hymns and would often stop pumping before Mrs Minett had finished playing, resulting in the organ producing a mournful din.

The Chapel's Sunday School was always well attended, and each week the register was marked. When the summer came, for those who had attended regularly, there would be the Cherry Orchard picnic. The children enjoyed games around the trees, and then sat in the shade, enjoying the picnic provided by the members of the Chapel.

My paternal great grand-father, Harry Sainsbury, looked after the Chapel. On Saturday evening he would go across and light the stoves in the Chapel and vestry, and refill the oil lamps, so that the members of the congregation, arriving for morning service, found a warm and inviting Chapel.

The Reverend Walter Povey, Minister of the Congregational Chapel, Back Street.

Above: My Father, Gordon Sainsbury, enjoying a donkey ride at Weston-super-Mare in 1929, during one of the trips organised by the Congregational and Methodist Chapels, during the summer.

2 The Methodist Chapel

The Methodist Chapel was opened in 1851 and was registered in the Hawkesbury Upton Mission. The building was valued at £180 and work began in 1850.

Building materials of stone, lime, and plaster were purchased from the quarries at Sodbury, and the haulage cost to bring the materials by horse and cart to Sherston was £1.8s.9d. All the money for the Chapel was raised by donations and loans, as the only income was the rent of fifty-two shillings per annum, raised from the adjoining cottages. In 1964 the cottages were sold for £460 and the money used to build a kitchen and lavatories. At the same time, electric heating was installed to replace the old coke stove.

Many lay preachers took the service at the chapel, including Mr Ayliffe from Acton Turville, who always managed to muddle the sermons, so carried away would he get with the story he was telling. On one such occasion he was telling the tale of Jonah and the Whale. As he got well into the story, the excitement in the congregation was building, when he said, "An' Jonah, he swallowed that whale". Silence; then a small voice from the congregation said, "That aint right, Mr Ayliffe". "Well, it be good 'nough for Sherston volk", came the reply.

Another time one of the children in the Sunday School class asked "How round is the world, Mr Ayliffe?". "Tis as round as a donkey's yud", he answered — *yud* being Wiltshire for head.

In 1878 the Reverend Morgan was the minister at the church, and it was he who started the Methodist Sunday School. The children who attended also joined in the Cherry Orchard picnic with members of the Congregational Chapel.

Opposite below: A view of Back Street taken in about 1905. There were many shops and trades here including Ernest Neal's bicycle repair shop, Mr Hanks, the tailor, Mr Harry Dapper, shoe maker, Mr H Mills, bus operator, Mr E Selwood, signwriter, Mr Goulding, butcher, Mr Satteley, watchmaker, Compton and Dickenson, carriers, and Mr Goulding's transport depot.
The name of Back Street was changed to Cliff Road in 1957.

Above: Left to right: Mr & Mrs Tom Ritchings and Mr Rice, outside one of the two cottages adjoining the Methodist Chapel in Grove Road. Below: The Methodist Chapel at the top of the steps known as Cuckoo's Nap.

3 The Baptist Chapel

The Baptist Chapel in Grove Road (Back Lane) was erected in 1837, and could seat a congregation of 150 people. In 1879 the Reverend Samuel Stubbings was the Baptist Minister.

The actual Chapel was sited in the front garden of two cottages that were there at this time. Inside the Chapel was the baptismal bath, where the act of total immersion took place.

After the closure of the Chapel, it was sold and used for storage for many years. Eventually it was demolished and a cottage built on the site.

The wedding of Mr & Mrs Harold Jobbins at the Baptist Chapel in 1929.

4 Church of the Holy Cross

The Church of the Holy Cross is of the late Norman style, and thought to have been built about 1170. However, on the east wall of the Church is a figure reputed to be the effigy of John Rattlebone. It is all that is left of a much earlier Saxon Church which existed at the time of the Norman Conquest. The attempt of antiquarians to point out that the figure is dressed in clerical vestments, and that the supposed life-saving tile clasped to a wound, is in fact a Bible, and other minor details, have had little effect on the people of Sherston.

It is quite possible that the Saxon Church was built, or renamed, by Canute when he was King, for he often built churches on the sites of his battles. The chief evidence to support this suggestion lies in the dedication to the Holy Cross, which was the same as the battle cry of those days.

The font in the Church is of Norman construction. However, its value has been diminished by slight alterations to its octagonal shape. The eight sides are believed to represent the eight people saved in The Ark from the Flood.

There is also a story concerning a chest and John Rattlebone's suit of armour, which was reported in the North Wiltshire *Herald* on 6 October 1933 as follows: "The chest was sold in April 1895 to Sackville Cresswell Esq. His nephew H. Pinkney Cresswell of Chipping Camden most generously gave the chest back to the Church in May 1929.

The chest, which dates from the 13th century, held the sacred vestments and vessels, and for many years the suit of armour which was reputed to have belonged to John Rattlebone. In the 1930s the Sunday School children were allowed to look at the armour occasionally, but it then mysteriously disappeared and has never been seen since.

The Reverend Walter Cecil Page was vicar at Sherston from 1923 to 1934, and is fondly remembered by many of Sherston's older generation. He was a very keen supporter of the village Cricket and Football teams, also of the Wolf Cub and Scout Troop, and many other organisations that were in the village at that time. He was a man with a keen interest in local history, and shared his findings and thoughts in the monthly Parish Magazine. From time to time, he would reprint items of interest about the Parish

Above: Church of the Holy Cross, Sherston Magna, 1915.

Left: The disputed effigy of Sherston's hero, John Rattlebone, or a worthy cleric?

that he had collected, always ending with "Your affectionate Vicar Cecil Page".

Every summer the Sunday School children and the members of the choir would be taken on their annual outing to Cherry Orchard. However, one year Reverend Page decided to break with tradition by hiring one of Mr Mills's charabancs, to take the children to Weston-Super-Mare. There was great excitement as many of the children had never seen the sea before. Eventually the day arrived, and Reverend Page later wrote "the fact that every member of the party got back safely, speaks volumes for the stamina of us all".

Perhaps it was the luxury of the brand new motor coach that had something to do with it, or the novelty of the beach, or the cricket match , or the temperature of 86°F in the shade, or all of these things that contributed to everyone having a wonderful day. Mrs Page sent a telegram of good wishes, which was read at dinner time. Then, when the clock was on the stroke of seven, the coach began its return journey.

In December 1938 the Parochial Church Council in the Parish of the Holy Cross, Sherston wrote to the Bishop of Bristol to ask permission that they might have the electric light installed in the Church to replace the acetylene gas fittings.

Above: Interior of the Church, c. 1910-15, showing the acetylene gas lights and, in the foreground, the octagonal font. In 1903 the pulpit was on the left of the aisle.

Left: The Reverend Walter Cecil Page, vicar of Sherston from 1923 to 1934, photographed c. 1920.

FESTIVALS & LEISURE

1 The Trinity Monday Fair and the Chocolate King

On the Sunday evening before Trinity Monday, the Fair and Shows would be waiting just outside the village, and when 7.00pm came and Church evensong had ended, the Fair would then be allowed to enter the village.

Everyone would be out waiting and watching, and well into the night the showmen would be working to set up all the rides and side-shows. By the Monday morning all would be ready, waiting for the school children to come and claim their free ride. The whole of the High Street would be taken up with such marvels as the Swing Boats and Chair-A-Planes; then over to the boxing booth where boxing skills were tested, all fairly refereed by Mr Jack Vining, the baker. Outside the school was the famous Cake-Walk, where, having paid your penny, you attempted to walk the cake walk, trying to be the one to stay on the longest as it swayed from side to side.

Further up the High Street stood a red and gold painted wagon – the Chocolate King. He would usually park his wagon outside Ironside House. Once settled, he would open a panel in the side of the wagon and begin his banter, drawing the crowds with his cries of "Who will give me a penny?". If you handed over your money, he may perhaps give you five or six bars of chocolate; but perhaps the next customer would not be so lucky and get only one or two – you never could tell. Then after a while, he would close the panel and wait an hour or two before starting over again.

Outside the Balcony House a small horse-drawn caravan would arrive, driven by Mr Brown. After removing his horse from the shafts, he would lead it down to the Carpenters Arms' paddock to graze. Meanwhile, Mrs Brown was busy lighting up her Primus stoves and getting out her galvanised baths to begin her business of making toffee apples, humbugs, and curled brandy snaps. She pulled the humbug mixture into long strips, before cutting it into equal lengths with a pair of scissors.

Outside the barber's shop, much to the annoyance of Mr Sheppard, stood the Galloping Horses, also the enormous fairground organ, all run by the power generated by Little Jimmy, the steam engine.

There were all kinds of amazing things to see and do — coconut shies, darts, skittles. Then there were the side-shows where, for a penny or two, you could go and look at such attractions as 'The World's Busiest Little People'. On entering the tent, you faced cages and cages of mice! Into the next tent, where you gazed upon the 'Amazing Leopard Skin Lady', and the artist who had no arms but could paint beautiful pictures using his feet.

This then was the Fair, and after two days it would pack up and move on. But there was always the thought that it would be back again next year...

The Trinity Monday Fair and Shows; photograph c 1930, looking north up the High Street.

2 The Beaufort Polo Team

In 1929 the first annual spring tournament of the Beaufort Polo Club took place at the polo grounds at Norton. In 1931 teams from the Royal Horse Guards, the Queen's Bays, and the 11th Hussar's were amongst teams competing.

The Tournament lasted for three days; admission charge to the public was two shillings, with teas and alcoholic refreshments being available.

A frequent visitor to the tournaments was the Maharajah Bahdur of Kashmir. The Maharajah and his party would stay at the Hare and Hounds Hotel at Westonbirt; some of the pupils at the nearby Westonbirt Girl's School were from Indian palaces. The Maharajah's team consisted of thirty-six polo ponies, together with their riders, the ponies having arrived several weeks earlier from India. Also included in the team would be the grooms, all chosen from the Maharajah's personal bodyguard. These grooms were a familiar sight in Sherston, wearing their golden slippers and silken jodhpurs.

Some of the customs of these men caused much amusement in the village. For instance, if they were to see a domestic cat, they would be terrified, as the fear of large cats in their own country was understandable.

They took particular care of their appearance, especially their beards, which often reached to their waists. However, if they were ever to be seen with the beard unrolled, they would take the scissors and cut it off!

The ponies were kept at several different stables, some at the Manor in Sherston. Captain Scott Douglas, who rode for the Scott's Greys, would be the perfect host to the Indian teams.

Most of the other ponies were kept at Mr Wilson's stables at Westonbirt. Next door to the stables the blacksmith had his forge, and by the side of this was the cookhouse, used by the Indian grooms. Their strange customs were noticed here also. They often had to slaughter lambs to cook, but if ever the shadow of anyone passed over the animal, they would refuse to eat the meat.

If any of the polo ponies unfortunately were injured and had to be destroyed, the grooms would refuse to let the animal go to the kennels at nearby Badminton. Instead, they would light a huge fire and cremate the animal and mourn its passing with prayer.

Two of the Maharajah Bahdur of Kashmir's personal body guards, who also acted as grooms for his polo ponies; photographed with Joe Minett in 1930; the photograph was taken by his friend (my father) Gordon Sainsbury.

3 The Beaufort Hunt Steeplechase: Alderton Race Day

Another occasion when the fairs and shows came to Sherston was Race Day. Once again, the High Street would be alive with crowds enjoying this special day.

The racecourse itself was at Alderton and was run under National Hunt Rules. It was a very important race meeting, as the winner of the Open race then qualified for the Grand National.

There were six races including the Alderton Selling Handicap Steeplechase, the Grittleton Novices Steeplechase, and the Sherston Handicap Steeplechase. The races were held in April, and on 1 April 1950 the Sherston Handicap was won by Major Hugh Wakefield's *Watercress II*, second place went to Lt-Col Collins's *Bamboozle*, and third place to Mrs Hew Carruthers's *Hurri-Bomber*. The winner received a prize of two hundred and fifty sovereigns, second place was awarded fifty sovereigns, and third, twenty-five sovereigns. The Duke of Beaufort would attend these race meetings accompanied by his sister, Lady Blanche Scott Douglas.

Any information on the horses and riders could be obtained from the famous racing tipster, Prince Monolulu. To get to the race course from Sherston, one cycled up Thompsons Hill to Mr Smith's farm at Common Wood. Here it would be safe to leave one's bicycle and continue on foot across the fields to Alderton.

On one occasion, the Duke of Windsor was competing and, having taken a fall at one of the hurdles, was heard to utter a string of oaths for which he later apologised.

Back in Sherston things were getting lively. The Thirsty Five would be sat outside the Forester's Arms tuning up to play the latest tunes. Spot Rice would be playing his banjo with his face blacked up like a minstrel. Another familiar sight on Race Day was the famous Lofty Brothers. Standing well over six feet tall, and dressed in top hat and tails, they would stroll up and down the street playing their guitars and singing to the crowds.

With a choice of seven public houses, a very happy atmosphere was guaranteed on Race Day!

Above: April 1932
The Beaufort Steeplchase.
Left to right: The Duke of Beaufort, Mr L H Taylor, the Earl of Westmoreland, Lady Blanche Scott Douglas, and Mr McKay.

Left: Lady Blanche and Mr Herbert Blagarve, April 1932.

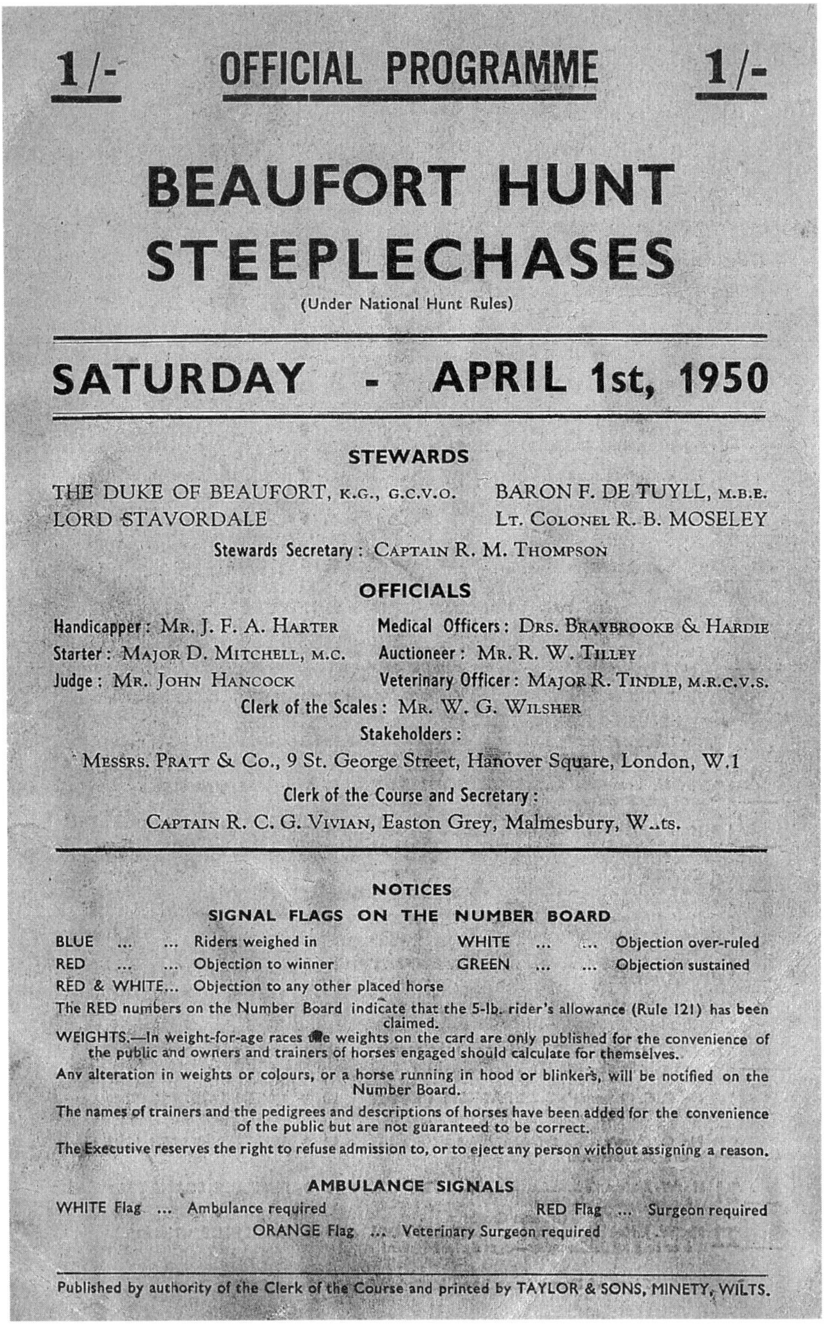

1/- OFFICIAL PROGRAMME 1/-

BEAUFORT HUNT STEEPLECHASES

(Under National Hunt Rules)

SATURDAY - APRIL 1st, 1950

STEWARDS

THE DUKE OF BEAUFORT, K.G., G.C.V.O.
BARON F. DE TUYLL, M.B.E.
LORD STAVORDALE
LT. COLONEL R. B. MOSELEY

Stewards Secretary: CAPTAIN R. M. THOMPSON

OFFICIALS

Handicapper: MR. J. F. A. HARTER
Medical Officers: DRS. BRAYBROOKE & HARDIE
Starter: MAJOR D. MITCHELL, M.C.
Auctioneer: MR. R. W. TILLEY
Judge: MR. JOHN HANCOCK
Veterinary Officer: MAJOR R. TINDLE, M.R.C.V.S.

Clerk of the Scales: MR. W. G. WILSHER

Stakeholders:

MESSRS. PRATT & CO., 9 St. George Street, Hanover Square, London, W.1

Clerk of the Course and Secretary:

CAPTAIN R. C. G. VIVIAN, Easton Grey, Malmesbury, W..ts.

NOTICES

SIGNAL FLAGS ON THE NUMBER BOARD

BLUE ... ... Riders weighed in
WHITE ... ... Objection over-ruled
RED ... ... Objection to winner
GREEN ... ... Objection sustained
RED & WHITE... Objection to any other placed horse

The RED numbers on the Number Board indicate that the 5-lb. rider's allowance (Rule 121) has been claimed.

WEIGHTS.—In weight-for-age races the weights on the card are only published for the convenience of the public and owners and trainers of horses engaged should calculate for themselves.

Any alteration in weights or colours, or a horse running in hood or blinkers, will be notified on the Number Board.

The names of trainers and the pedigrees and descriptions of horses have been added for the convenience of the public but are not guaranteed to be correct.

The Executive reserves the right to refuse admission to, or to eject any person without assigning a reason.

AMBULANCE SIGNALS

WHITE Flag ... Ambulance required
RED Flag ... Surgeon required
ORANGE Flag ... Veterinary Surgeon required

Published by authority of the Clerk of the Course and printed by TAYLOR & SONS, MINETY, WILTS.

Official Programme for the Beaufort Hunt Steeplechases. 1 April 1950

4 Queen Elizabeth II's Coronation Day

On 2 June 1953 the village celebrated the Coronation of Queen Elizabeth II. The High Street was decorated with bunting, and the schoolchildren had a fancy dress parade. Shopkeepers in the village were invited to enter a competition for the best-dressed window.

To celebrate the occasion, the Parish council ordered two gross of decorated china mugs at a cost of 18/6d per dozen. These mugs were then given to every child in the village.

Above: Queen Elizabeth II's Coronation Day parade. Mrs Cooper is standing in the doorway of The Foresters' Arms Inn. Mrs Mary Price is walking beside the schoolchildren.
Below: Gordon and Peggy Sainsbury's (my parents) hardware shop window, in Back Street, decorated for the Coronation.

5 The Sherston Town Band

'Now thun, Bert, thee watch they snotty black 'uns, an I'll put they twiddly bits in!'

In 1884 the Salvation Army was holding regular meetings at the home of Mr John Clarke, the village Fellmonger, who lived in the Tan House on Tanners Hill.

It was probably the sound of the Army's band that prompted Mr Clarke's sons, Ernest, Bert, and Ambrose, to form a band of their own, and so the first Sherston Brass and Reed Band was started. Well turned out in their smart uniforms and under the leadership of Ernest, the band would play at all the events that took place in the village from about 1912.

However, it is from about 1925 that most memories of the band are recalled; with any mention of the Thirsty Five bringing a smile to the faces of old Sherstonians. They will all grin and say, "I can remember the night they played to the hay rick". It appears that the Thirsty Five were not averse to taking a drop or two of the 'hard' stuff, and were especially partial to Farmer Thomson's Plum Jerkum. On this particular night, they had been out wassailing and had decided to walk to Sopworth to play their carols and — if offered — partake of a seasonal tipple. They began their return journey and decided to take a break and play a few more tunes to the 'big house', then to knock at the door. It was then that they discovered it was the hay rick that they had been serenading!

There was also some doubt as to whether the men could actually read music, as on more than one occasion, it was noticed that their sheet music was upside down on the music stand. Their selection of music was also rather limited as, when asked what they could play, the reply would be, "Well, there's this 'un, thak 'un, an t'other".

In the summer months the village held Penny Hop dances in the High Street, and, sat behind the railings of the Forester's Arms Inn, the Thirsty Five would be tuning up. Ernest would be twiddling his moustache, and moistening his lips with his beer. At the end of the evening he would say, "Now then Bert, what shall we finish wi?", and Bert would reply, "Well, we've played this 'un all night, and they seemed to like it, so we's might as well end wi it".

And so, whenever there was a need for music in the village, the Thirsty Five could be depended on to provide it, even though they might have to be carried home at the end. On one occasion Bumper Gough's big bass drum, which was almost as big as the man himself, was seen rolling down Tanners Hill with Bumper in hot pursuit. Though sadly all the members of the band are dead, happy memories of their music and tuning up outside the Forester's Arms linger on.

Above: Sherston Town Brass & Reed Band, photographed by Mr Ernest Neal between 1905-10. Though few of the members' names are recorded, we do know that Hector (Hec) Rice is in the back row, fourth from left, and George Hill, the band's conductor and local baker, is seated in the centre holding his cornet.

Left: Hec Rice holding Arthur Palmer, in 1937.

6 The Pennymead: Sherston Recreation Field

Up until the early 1930s the children of the village used a field down Sopworth Lane to play football and cricket. Then in 1933 a plot of land belonging to the Stroud Breweries became available to buy. The field was known locally as the Pennymead and was thought to be the remains of old Roman earthworks.

Ideally situated at Court Street and close to the village school, it was a perfect site to build a playing field. And so, with the help of an interest-free loan from Mrs Bert Compton, the land was purchased for £100, on condition that if it ever came up for sale again, first refusal to buy it would be given to Stroud Breweries.

The field itself was very uneven, but during the war the American servicemen stationed at Pinkney Park kindly used their heavy earth-moving equipment to level it, much to the amusement of the villagers.

To repay the loan, events were organised, including the village carnival. The Sherston Recreation Ground Committee (SRGC) was formed and the carnival queen and her attendants proudly wore blue sashes, on which were printed the SRGC initials, as they rode on the back of Mr Wilson's coal lorry for the parade. The queen was chosen by whoever sold the most carnival tickets – a penny each – and in 1934 this was Betty Dickenson, with Kath Bishop, Joan Howard, and Rosemary Webb as her attendants. The carnival parade was judged by Lady Blanche Scott Douglas from The Manor.

The Recreation Ground was officially opened by Lady Rosemary Elliot (Lady Blanche's daughter) on Jubilee day. There was a large crowd at the ceremony and before the red, white and blue ribbon was cut, the National Anthem was sung. Mr Warren, the school's headmaster, assisted in the ceremony, and Miss Vera Butler presented Lady Rosemary with a posy of flowers. Afterwards the school children gave displays of physical drill and the Girl Guides and Brownies entertained. There were football matches and a tug-of-war for the adults, dancing, fireworks, and the release of two paper balloons, and a huge bonfire to complete the day.

The fund raising continued. Mr Walt (Sonny) Compton kept greyhounds, and, together with Roy Sainsbury, built a small race track in the Pennymead, complete with a rag rabbit for the dogs to chase. To advertise the event, Sonny and Roy walked around wearing top hats and frock coats, and carrying placards declaring "If you want to have some fun, come and watch the greyhounds run", and "Gone to the dogs". No doubt several bets would have been placed on the dogs, with all the profits going to the fund to repay the loan and provide equipment for the children.

In 1935, for the children's safety, the walls around the Pennymead were rebuilt. A stone plaque is inset in the wall bearing the names of H Sherwood, P Snell, and H Evans who donated their time to the wall's renovation.

When the recreation field was first opened, the gates were unlocked at sunrise and locked again at sunset. This task was done by Mr E Neal (Ern Curly), who lived nearby.

In 1963, after careful consideration and their goal having been achieved, the Recreation Ground Committee was disbanded and the upkeep of the play-field was passed on to the Parish Council.

Sherston Recreation Ground carnival, 1934. Left to right: Kath Bishop, Betty Dickenson, Joan Howard, Rosemary Webb (seated foreground)

'Gone to the Dogs': Left to right: Roy Sainsbury, Peter Dickenson and Walt Compton, 1934.

Trades & Commerce

Men at Work, 1895.
Men working for the Parish at the turning into Sandpits Lane. Mr Blackmore Senior is at the rear of the picture. The bowler-hatted gentleman in front is Mr Dickenson.

In the 1930s Mr Neal lived at the house in the photograph. He used the shed opposite to repair pots, pans, kettles and the like. He also had the title of Saw Doctor, as he repaired and sharpened saws.

Opposite: The mill pool and hatches on the opposite side of the road to the mill and looking towards Luckington, photographed from the Cliff, c. 1910.

Above: The corn mill (left) at the bottom of Brook Hill, c. 1910, and the Silk Mill (right). The large white marquee, in front of the silk mill, was owned by the Evangelist Society from London, whose members made regular visits to the village.

1 Sherston Silk Mills

The Silk Mill, situated at the bottom of Brook Hill, was erected in 1872 and was the business premises of Joseph Davenport & Son, who at the same time owned the larger silk mills at Malmesbury.

The Silk Mill brought very welcome employment to many people in the village, including those that had left school aged 14. The Mill manufactured silks and ribbons. At the end of each day the young girls at the Mill would take home all the off-cuts of silk to hem into handkerchiefs. In 1894 the Mill passed into the ownership of Daniel Darling & Co with Alfred Lister as manager. By this time cotton material, as well as silk, was being produced.

In 1902 Alfred Parkinson, a native of Yorkshire, went into partnership with Mr Lister, where they continued in business together until 1922. When the Mill finally closed, the looms and machinery were sold to the Malmesbury Mill, where many of the weavers also went to work, cycling there and back every day.

Since then, many uses have been found for the mill buildings. One of the persons to have owned them was Herbert Goulding, who was originally employed at the Mill for a few shillings a week. He left Sherston, failed and prospered in a number of occupations, but returned to Sherston where he purchased the Mill for 'a song', and in which he kept pigs.

Other businesses, including paint manufacturers, engineering works, and a cattle cake mill for the Wiltshire farmers, have all used the mill site. After lying vacant for several years and falling into disrepair, its life has turned full circle, and in 1969 it was purchased by Tubbs Elastics, and once again, the sounds of looms weaving fabric can be heard.

Opposite: Sherston Silk Mill workers; 21 December 1905.
Alfred Lister, senior partner, is (standing) in the third row on the left. Alfred Parkinson is on the extreme right of the photograph. In the back row, on the left is my great grandfather, Harry Sainsbury; next to him is Mr Dickenson; amongst the others are Alf Neal, W and Harry Ball, Mr Peters, Liza Taylor, and Omar Neal. Mrs Gough is in the second row, and Alice Neal and Mrs Jobbins are amongst the ladies in the fornt row. Seated on the ground, second from left, is Arthur (Slen) Neale; my grandfather, Vernon Sainsbury, is next to him, and Wilfred Lighthowler, Secretary, is on the right.

Above: Inside the Silk Mill, 1905.
Left to right standing: 3rd, S Dickenson; 7th, Mr Peters; extreme right, Mr Ball.

2 The Sherston Co-operative Milling Society

In 1086, when the Domesday Book was compiled, and all land and buildings were entered for tax purposes, Sherston was recorded as having two Grist Mills, both owned by the Lord of the Manor. A mill in those days would have been a very valuable possession, as everyone needed to have their corn ground.

One of these mills stood at the bottom of Thompsons Hill in the field next to the river. The other one was at the bottom of Brook Hill. It was at the end of the 1800s that this mill became the property of a group of people who formed the Co-Operative Milling Society, with shares being available to anyone who wished to invest.

The mill was run by water power, with the flow of the water being regulated by the hatches which were situated at the other side of the road, the fast flowing water turning the massive grinding stones. The corn ground at the mill was usually purchased from the various farms around Sherston, but also came from other locations.

The Great Western Railway Company carried maize, barley, and oats from Portishead, Bristol, and Avonmouth, and delivered them to Badminton Station, where the mill's horse and cart would be waiting to bring the load back to Sherston. These goods were all paid for from the Petty Cash and meticulously recorded in the Day book. In 1910 some of these were:

J Styles & Miles, Grocers	10 sacks of beans at 16s.6d. per sack
Mr Henry Pritchard	11 sacks and 21/2 Bushels of Oats £4.18.10d.
Mr GW Daniels	10 sacks of beans at 16s.6d.
The GWR Company	£6.14.1d. carriage charges

Wages were also recorded in the Day Book. In 1908 the average day's wage for the miller was 2s.6d., and in 1909, Miss Mary Anne Evans, the secretary, received her quarterly salary of £2.0s.0d. Mr Brinkworth received £1.6s.0d in payment of the Malmesbury Union Parish Poor Rate. Other office items were purchased including envelopes costing 4d., stamps at 1s.0d., a telegram for 6d., and blotting paper for 2d.

Another main expense was maintenance of the mill's transport, namely the horse. Mr Arthur Merchant, the village blacksmith, paid regular calls to the mill, and in January 1921 he was paid 13s.6d. for shoeing the horse. Mr Phillips, the saddler, was paid £1.13s.9d. for repairs to the harness, and 4s.0d. to Duncan Neale, the veterinary surgeon, for horse drench.

From the early 1920s Mr CW Ball was manager at the mill, and in 1923, after closure of the silk mill nearby, Mr AL Parkinson became Secretary.

The corn mill continued in business until the early 1950s when it was eventually purchased by the Wiltshire Farmers. Nothing now remains of the old mill house or the sheds that were used to store the ground corn.

The mill pond at the bottom of Brook Hill, on the opposite side of the road to the mill.

Mr Billy Thompson, photographed in 1930, watching the water rushing through the hatches. The hatch gates regulated the flow of water driving the mill wheel.

Above: A view of the mill house and, on the opposite side of the road, the sheds where the corn and flour were stored, c. 1930.

Left: The second, and smaller, grist mill at the bottom of Thompsons Hill, owned in 1930, when this photograph was taken, by Oliver Lydiard.

Opposite: The only water standpipe remaining in Sherston.

3 Sherston Parish Water Works

'Water, water, everywhere – but not a drop to spare.'

Before 1904 water was collected from the river springs and sold from the back of a horse and cart for a ha'penny per pint. The Parish Council then decided to build a windmill on the site of the present-day water works.

The windmill's job was to send large leather buckets down a deep bore hole to the underground rivers. It was then pumped along pipes to feed all the stand-pipes situated around the village. Many people already had their own wells, but when a long dry period was experienced, they were more than grateful to be able to go and fill their buckets from the stand-pipes.

Mr Ernest Neal took care of the windmill, as well as keeping a smallholding in the fields nearby. Here he kept a small herd of cows which provided him with a good supply of milk and which he sold from his house in Back Street. His other interests included painting in water colours and photography — many of the photographs in this book are taken by him in the early part of the 1900s. In his later years, he ran a bicycle repair shop in Back Street.

In the 1930s Bristol Water Board decided to build water works at Shipton Moyne, some five miles east of Sherston. Sherston's water supply was severely depleted and the pressure dropped dramatically. Since Sherston was at a higher ground level than Shipton Moyne, there seemed to be only one solution — to make the Sherston bore hole much deeper. Unfortunately, the Parish Council could not raise the necessary funds needed for such a large development, and there was no alternative but to sell to the Water Board.

There is now only one of the original standpipes left in the village, and that is down at Forlorn — albeit, minus its helmet!

Above: Mr Ernest Neal leaning on his bicycle, c. 1915.

Below: One of the standpipes, placed around the village in 1904, in front of the Jubilee Tree; photograph c. 1935.

4 Sewage!

Up until the late 1940s the houses in the village relied on their old outside water closets and cesspools. However, in 1951 an application was made on behalf of Malmesbury Rural District Council for a grant under the Rural Water Supplies and Sewage Act of 1944 to lay sewage pipes in Noble Street, the High Street, and Back Street.

At this time there were approximately 387 properties in the village. The estimated cost of the scheme was £4,593. Work commenced on 11 March 1952 and was finally completed in September. In 1954 another application for a grant was made amounting to £17,600 for the laying of a new Outfall Sewer and construction of a new sewage waste disposal works.

The field in the background was known as the Tarters (and the housing estate built on the site bears its name). The sewage works were built in the valley at the bottom of the hill to the right of the picture; photographed in 1935.

5 The Herb Collectors

Parsley, Sage, Rosemary and Thyme.

Mint, great and lesser celandine, dandelion root, violet leaves, St John's wort, sorrel, pigwort, comfrey, ragwort, wood sage, and nettles were all collected by women in Sherston. These herbs were then inspected for quality, species and dryness before the Herbwoman, who acted for a large herb merchant at Sutton Benger, came to pay her workers.

The price varied considerably for different species, from two to three pence per pound, to up to half-a-crown a pound.

One of these herb collectors in Sherston was Mrs Lizzie Clarke who lived at the bottom of Bustlers Hill. She would collect the herbs from the fields and hedgerows, and put them in her sack-like apron tied around her waist. She then took them home where they would be sorted and laid out to dry on her shed roof.

In Lizzie's shed there was a large double-burner paraffin stove, and it was on this that she made her home-made faggots, no doubt tastily seasoned with her herbs.

The horse splash at the bottom of Tanners Hill. Three different families lived here, including Mrs Butler, who was an herb collector, drying her herbs over netting placed along the walls. In the background is Clarke's Tannery; photographed c. 1935.

6 The Undertaker

Mr Blackmore, Mr Bignell, and later Mr Harold Jobbins were all Undertakers in the village. When a person passed away the undertaker was called to make all the arrangements, often with Mrs Neal to assist in the laying-out of the body.

On one occasion Mrs Neal had seen to an old gentleman in the village who had just died. She washed and dried the body, and then, turning to his wife, she asked if she had a clean shirt she could put on him. The old lady, who was obviously upset, replied, "Oh!, I have, but it aint aired".

Another lady asked Mr Jobbins, who was the undertaker from 1933-64, to come and see to the arrangements for her husband who had just died. As was the custom, the body was placed in the coffin and left in the front room until the day of the funeral. Mrs Neal would visit each day to make sure all was all right with the corpse. The day of the funeral came, and Mr Jobbins and his assistants went to place the lid on the coffin, calling for the lady to come and say her last 'Goodbye'. She came into the room carrying his pipe and tobacco, some coins, and a blanket for his journey. She then said her farewell.

This same old lady kept two candles lit in her front room window every evening. When asked why she did this, she replied that during the First World War her two sons had been reported missing, presumed dead, and that she kept the candles lit to show them the way home. They never returned.

Mr Harold Jobbins, undertaker from 1933 to 1964.

7 The Barber

"Short back and sides, please"

If you ask any old Sherstonian about the shops in the village, nearly all of them will mention Barber Jack. Mr Jack Sheppard had his first barber's establishment in a shed in the school field. Later he moved to new premises in the High Street.

He was a very strict Baptist and forbade the use of bad language, spitting, and blasphemy in his shop, and just to make sure this was upheld, he had notices on the walls to remind his clients. There was also a large banner proclaiming *The wages of sin are death.* As one entered the shop, there stood a large lectern on which lay a Bible, opened at the appropriate Lesson of the day.

In front of his leather barber's chair was a massive speckled mirror, reflecting not only the seated client but also displays of bottles, tins of hair tonics and brilliantine. A haircut would cost $1\frac{1}{2}$d. and if you required a shave as well, it would cost 2d. If shaving his client, Jack would sharpen his cut-throat razor on a strop hanging on the wall, lather well with the shaving soap, and proceed to shave.

Mr Jack Sheppard, gentlemen's hairdresser.

Daily newspapers were also available at Jack's, as he was the village newsagent. Saturday mornings were usually the busiest day for the barber, but on one particular Saturday, business was unusually quiet. Jack left his shop to go to the Post Office, and on his return he realised the reason why. Tied to his railings there was a large notice: "Closed. Gone to Chepstow races". Most people had a good idea as to who had played the practical joke, but I do not know if anyone ever told Barber Jack!

8 Health Care

Over the past one hundred years the village has seen many changes to the health care of the villagers. Up until the late 1950s the doctor's surgery was at the Doctor's house in Easton Town. Some of the past General Practitioners have included Dr Edwin Smith in 1865, Dr WR Tollerton in 1879, Dr Edward Hunt in 1903, Dr James Robinson Fletcher in 1907, Dr J Jones in 1930, and Dr J Woods in 1939.

Miss Elizabeth Woods, the Doctor's daughter, bred prize-winning Bull Terriers, and owned a boarding kennel business, called The Wooden Kennels, which she ran from the garden of her father's house.

Sister Mary Anne Lewis was the District Nurse from the late 1920s. Because there was no National Health Service in those days, people paid into the nurse's fund, especially young married couples who were considering starting a family. The fund then ensured that, at the time of the confinement, all expenses would be paid. Towards the end of the 1950s, the surgery moved to the Swan Barton where Dr Titherton took over from Dr Woods.

If one needed dental treatment the place to go would be the Angel Hotel where Mr Loxton, from Bristol, attended on Wednesday evenings. If the patient was unfortunate enough to need an extraction, it would cost half-a-crown. Mr Alfred Soar also attended to dental care on the second and last Thursday of each month and treated his patients in Mr Mills's shoe shop.

The doctor's house and surgery (in the fore-ground) at Easton Town, c. 1940. His tennis court can be seen alongside the house.

9 Mr Duncan Neale: Chemist and Veterinary Surgeon

In 1933 the death occurred of Mr Duncan Neale, who was a well-known landowner and gentleman of the village. Together with his older brother, Moses, they ran the village chemist's shop. They were also veterinary surgeons, as their father had been before them, and were engaged in the manufacturing of sheep dip.

At the time of his death, his wife went to the village undertaker and asked if he would make the necessary arrangements, but not to bother making a coffin as he already had one under the bed. Several stories are still told in the village concerning Duncan Neale's coffin — that he used to take his afternoon nap in it, and that he kept it on a pair of trestles in the dining room.

On 22 June 1934 Duncan Neale bequeathed £200 to the Trustees of the Iddols Charity, stipulating that they were to provide relief to the poor of the village by donating a bag of coal in winter. The Trust fund is still in use, but very little is left of the original £200.

Mr Neale was also a Senior Juror of the Ancient Court Leet, and his services were called upon in 1914 when, at the last meeting of the Parish Council, a resolution was passed prohibiting the annual Trinity Monday roundabouts and shows from staying longer than the Monday night. The villagers were most annoyed, to say the least, that such an enjoyable tradition should be restricted to a single day.

The Parish Council's resolution was reported to the Lord of the Manor, who called for a Court Leet to be convened. It was agreed that the rights and traditions of the village should be preserved, and the Lord of the Manor instructed the Bailiff to grant permission to the owners of the shows for their stay in the village to last until the Tuesday evening. This Order of the Court then had to be confirmed in public.

At 6.00pm a procession formed at the Jubilee tree, consisting of children, Sherston Town Band, and almost all the people of the village. Headed by the Jury, they then proceeded to Mr Cole, the owner of the shows.

It was then that Duncan Neale mounted the platform before the assembled crowd and called for order. After the cheering had

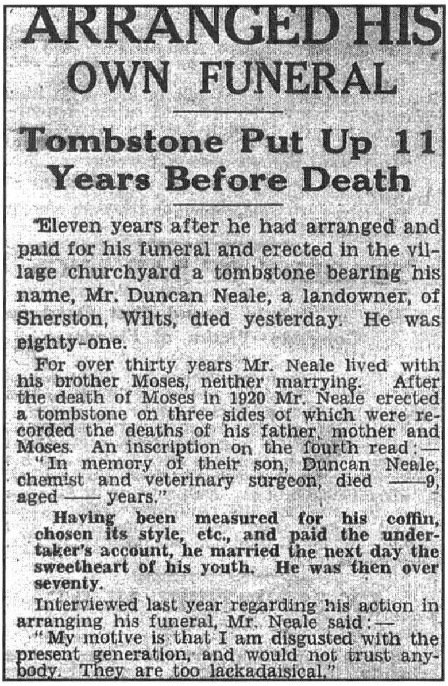

ARRANGED HIS OWN FUNERAL

Tombstone Put Up 11 Years Before Death

Eleven years after he had arranged and paid for his funeral and erected in the village churchyard a tombstone bearing his name, Mr. Duncan Neale, a landowner, of Sherston, Wilts, died yesterday. He was eighty-one.

For over thirty years Mr. Neale lived with his brother Moses, neither marrying. After the death of Moses in 1920 Mr. Neale erected a tombstone on three sides of which were recorded the deaths of his father, mother and Moses. An inscription on the fourth read:—

"In memory of their son, Duncan Neale, chemist and veterinary surgeon, died ——9, aged —— years."

Having been measured for his coffin, chosen its style, etc., and paid the undertaker's account, he married the next day the sweetheart of his youth. He was then over seventy.

Interviewed last year regarding his action in arranging his funeral, Mr. Neale said:—

"My motive is that I am disgusted with the present generation, and would not trust anybody. They are too lackadaisical."

Newspaper extract recording the strange tale of Duncan Neale's funeral, 1933.

died down he continued: "With your usual good order, our Bailiff will open the Court". Mr Hill, the Bailiff, rang his bell three times and read: "Oyez, oyez, oyez. Please take notice, gentlemen of the Jury of the Court Leet and Court Baron of Charles Richard Estcourt Cresswell, Lord of the Manor of Sherston Magna, I, the sworn Bailiff, did receive a letter from you through Mr Duncan Neale pointing out the ancient rights and traditions of the Ancient Manor of Sherston Magna. And you did exercise the power vested in me to give the Shows permission to stay this Trinity Tuesday night. The terms to be the same as last year, a free ride for all the school children."

Mr Duncan Neale then addressed the crowds and said: "To the inhabitants of this Ancient Parish of Sherston Magna, and as a Juryman and on behalf of the Jurymen standing here for the Court Leet and Court Baron of Charles Richard Estcourt Cresswell Esquire for the Manor of Sherston, I do swear the statements just made to be the truth, the whole truth, and nothing but the truth, so help me God." The proceedings then ended with the singing of the National Anthem.

Mr Duncan Neale's Pharmacy Shop is in the High Street, and is a most unusual looking house. On close inspection, the initial 'N' can be seen on the pillars either side of the front of the house. An unusual house for a very unusual man.

The tombstone of Thomas, Moses and Duncan Neale.

10 Zachariah Satteley 1820-1897: Watch and Clockmaker

"If you vant a vatch, buy a vatch –stop looking in my vindee!"

Zachariah Satteley was born in Baden in 1820 and came to Sherston as a British subject some time in the mid-1800s. He met and married his wife Susan (née Berry), who was born in Sherston, and together they began their watch and clock-making business in Back Street.

They had four children; George was born in 1853, William in 1856, Emma in 1859, and Albert in 1861. The four children all learnt the trade of watchmaker, and it was William who carried on the family business in Sherston, after the death of his father in 1897.

Zachariah Satteley did not appreciate window-shoppers, and dealt with them abruptly: "If you vant a vatch, buy a vatch — stop looking in my vindee!"

There are a few Satteley clocks remaining, and the one I tracked down, illustrated here, is a handsome example of a wooden wall clock bearing the inscription *Satteley & Sons Sherston*. Interestingly, Zachariah and Susan's tomb stone shows their name spelt *Sattely*.

Left: One of the few Satteley clocks remaining in Sherston.

Opposite: Sherston Post Office with the letterbox in the wall to the left of the shop window; Sherston's first red telephone box was to the right of the shop door.

11 Sherston Post Office

Mr Harry P Dicks was the sub-postmaster and ran this service from his Drapery and Grocery shop at Cheltenham House, which stands at the southern end of the High Street, at the top of Brook Hill. Here one could send Telephonic Express Deliveries (telegrams) to destinations within a limited distance. Visitors to Sherston could buy and send picture postcards of the village from Mr Dicks's shop. Many of the photographs in this book are reproductions of these old postcards. The cost of a postage stamp for cards was 1/2d, and collections were made at 2.45pm and 6.40pm, and on Sundays at 11.50am.

The first red telephone box was outside the Post Office. One day an unfortunate child managed to get stuck between the box and the wall, and freeing him and was a major problem.

In later years, after the Post Office had moved to the opposite end of the High Street, Mr Dicks's daughter, with the assistance of Miss Stinchcomb, managed the Grocery and Drapery shop. Here one could buy household linen, undergarments, dresses, hats, shoes, haberdashery, and virtually anything that was needed. The long wooden counter stretched from one end of the shop to the other, with chairs on which to sit whilst making one's purchases.

At the far end of the shop were the grocery items — huge tin cans filled with tea, sugar, rice — all waiting to be weighed and bagged. Miss Dicks and Miss Stinchcomb kept the drapery shop going until the late 1950s when it eventually closed. Many villagers remember this particular shop with great affection.

Above: Miss Dicks's Haberdashery and Post Office, c. 1945; just visible, top right hand side of the photograph, are the picture postcards of the village that she sold. The post office section was half-way down the counter, behind the screen, where the letter scales can be seen.

12 Mr Herbert (Corky) Smith: Village Tailor

Henry Hanks, together with his son Mark, carried out their gentleman's tailoring trade from their shop in Back Street. They also passed on their skills to apprentice tailors. One of these was Mr Herbert Smith, who eventually went on to be the village tailor from 1920 to 1970.

Mr Smith was affectionately known as *Corky*, and for fifty years he ran his Gents Tailors from his shop at the far end of the High Street, next door to Miss Dicks's store.

A familiar sight was Mr Smith, sitting cross-legged in his shop window, hand-sewing the buttonholes on the gentlemen's suits that he was making. From the room at the back of his shop he sold gentlemen's hosiery and undergarments, and in later years, even Wellington boots. All the young men of the village had their best Sunday suits made by Corky.

Even though Corky was a 'Chapel man', he still had a sense of humour. One evening one of the village lads painted a sign on Corky's shop window which read: *BEER IS BEST*. The next day Corky had added to it: *LEFT ALONE!*

Opposite: The village Post Office Stores belonging to Mr Dicks, c. 1930. To the right is Herbert (Corky) Smith's tailor's shop. The window to the left of the door is where Corky would sit, to get the best light, and sew the buttonholes in the suits he made.
On the extreme right of the picture is a bicycle leaning against the wall of George Evans's bicycle repair shop. He worked up a narrow alley that ran between the cottages.

13 Carriers

In 1921 Bert Compton was registered as Fishmonger and Carrier, operating from Thompsons Hill. In 1923 he joined forces with Walt Dickenson. Over seventy years later, Compton and Dickenson are still operating today with their depot located in Sandpits Lane.

Above: Roy Sainsbury, Walt Dickenson and Bert Compton with their first lorries in the yard at Thompsons Hill, c. 1925.

Left: Mr E Horton beside his Chevrolet lorry in Noble Street, c. 1930. Mr Horton travelled to Bristol, Malmesbury and Tetbury.

14 John Styles and Thomas Miles: Grocers

Styles and Miles Grocery shop was at the bottom of Easton Town. Established in 1850 it was reputed to be the largest of the shops in the village, where just about anything could be bought.

Mr Miles also ran a small farm from the fields behind the shop, and it was his freshly slaughtered livestock that would be on sale at the butcher's counter in the shop.

The shop continued in the Miles' family for many years.

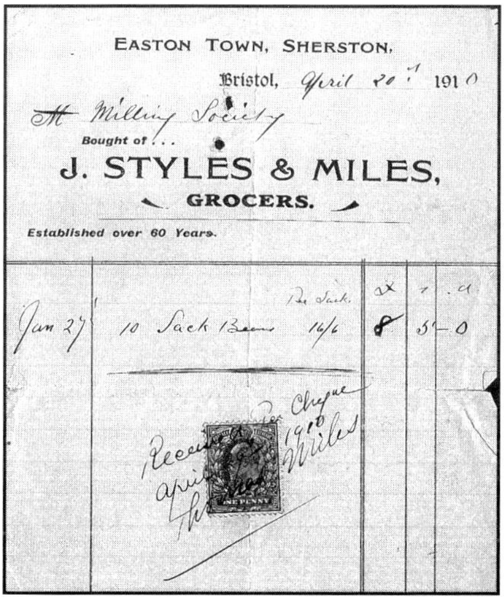

EASTON TOWN, SHERSTON.

Bristol, April 20th 1910

Milling Society

Bought of . . .

J. STYLES & MILES,

GROCERS.

Established over 60 Years.

		Per Sack			
Jan 27	10 Sack Bran	16/6	8	5	0

Received per Cheque April 1910 Thos Miles

Above: Alf Miles standing in the road in front of Styles and Miles Provision Merchants, 1910.

Above: Sherston High Street, c. 1970. Notice the two antique shops; there were approximately eight other shops in the village at the time. Below: Mrs Eva Dore in the doorway of her husband's shop, which they ran in the 1930s. The house itself, recently called Draper's Rest, was reputedly built in 1683. Mr Dore's window display included jars of sweets, bunches of bananas, cards of combs and hairgrips, paint brushes, and advertised Puritan soap, Soako, and Lyons tea – very much a general store.

Mrs Camm outside her husband's grocery shop in the High Street. One of the rhymes about the shopkeepers, recited by children of the village went:
Billy Camm said, "We've sold out of ham,"
Tom Dore said, "We got no more,"
George Platt said, "I've shot the cat."
Billy Camm delivered groceries around the village in his horse and trap. One day the horse was startled and careered into the shop window of Corky Smith's tailor's shop.

15 The Sands Hatchery

Mr George Smith purchased The Sands in Sandpits Lane in 1921. He installed incubators in the sheds, and it was not long before the Sands Hatchery became a thriving business, with hundreds of day-old chicks being despatched all over the country, as far afield as Yorkshire and Wales. Then disaster struck with the country's General Strike in 1926. Week after week there were no trains and Mr Smith could not get the necessary food for the chickens as they hatched. Inevitably, this lead to the end of the Hatchery.

The Orchard continued to produce a good supply of apples, pears, plums, greengages, strawberries and raspberries. The apples were sold at 1d. per pound, or 1/2d. for fall-downs, and plums at 2d. per pound.

16 Mr W (Billy) Thompson: Greengrocer & Fishmonger

Mr Thompson had his first greengrocer's shop at the top of the Swan Barton. In about 1935 he moved to premises in the High Street. *The Laurels* had a large shop window where he displayed his fruit and vegetables. Before daybreak, Billy would set off for Bristol fish market in his Chrysler motor van, which had been customised to hold the boxes of fish packed in ice that he had purchased from the market.

During the late fifties, he moved again to Grove Road, where he continued to run his business. By now he had gone 'mobile', delivering all round the village several days a week. The most familiar memory of Billy was on a Saturday afternoon in his white overall, blowing a hunting horn to let everyone know he was about!

Left: Billy announcing his arrival, c. 1960.
Below: Billy outside his in-laws' house in the High Street, 1943.

Mr Frank Thompson & Son: Bakers

From 1869 until 1914 Mr J Elsip was Baker and Miller at the Bakehouse at the top of Brook Hill, the building that housed the ovens having been built in 1723. He was then succeeded by Mr Frank Thompson.

It was when Mr Thompson took over that the tradition of baking the village's Christmas cakes began. Because the average household oven was not sturdy enough to endure the long process of baking a rich fruit cake. So every year, the women would make their cake, wrap it well with thick brown paper, label it, then take it to Mr Thompson who would put it in his bread ovens. The ovens could bake up to forty cakes at a time. Frank Thompson also cooked many a Sherston family's turkey; the bird being taken to his ovens, still hot from baking bread, on Christmas Day!

The flour used for the bread was milled at the bottom of Brook Hill by the Sherston Co-Operative Milling Society. Ready-milled flour could also be bought at the bakehouse.

The shop window of the bakery faced on to Brook Hill, and every morning, displayed on cake stands, would be all the freshly-made confectioneries, including Mr Thompson's famous lardie cake.

Miss Dix and Mrs Thompson delivered daily around the village, first by hand-cart, and pony and trap to the surrounding villages; later a motorised van was used. The bread orders were carried in large wicker baskets and delivered to the door. The two ladies continued to make their rounds until the late 1960s when the bakehouse finally closed with the retirement of Mr Sam Thompson.

THOMAS ELSIP,
Baker, Mealman,
CORN AND FLOUR DEALER,
HIGH STREET,
SHERSTON.

Above: Left to right: Miss Dix, Chris Berry, Frank Thompson, Sam Thompson and Mrs Gladys Thompson, with their array of vehicles at the back of the bakehouse, c. 1925.
Below: Mr & Mrs Frank Thompson outside the bakery shop in about 1925. The steam engine belonging to Hancock's Haulage had broken down on Brook Hill, causing great interest.

Above: Mr Thompson and Sam making deliveries to Easton Town in about 1928.

Below: Mr Thompson in his new car at the back of the bakery, c. 1935.

18 WJ Vining: Baker & Confectioner

From about 1860 the Hill family ran the bakery that was situated behind the Tolsey. Henry Hill was succeeded by his son, George, who carried on the business until about 1927. It was then that Mr and Mrs Vining took over the bakehouse. Until this time, Mr Vining had been employed by Major K Menzies at Easton Town farm as his chef.

Mr and Mrs Vining continued their bakery until the 1970s. After their deaths, they were both laid to rest in the Congregational Chapel's graveyard, where Mr Vining's headstone is in the form of a loaf of bread.

Left: Walt Neal delivering orders for Mr Vining, c. 1935

Opposite above: George Evans's Garage; Front: Fred Evans is on the left, with Billy Thompson holding his son's hand.

Opposite below: On the right is Maurice Bishop's shop in Back Street, 1895. Mr Bishop was a fishmonger and potato merchant, and lived at Cuckoo's Nap.

19 Mr George Evans's Garage

Mr George Evans ran his automobile garage next to the Carpenter's Arms public house from the early 1920s.

Mr Evans also had a generator, so when the accumulator for anyone's wireless was running low, they went to the garage to have them charged.

In the late thirties, the new GEC electric wireless was available and, as Mr Evans had a small shop at the side of the garage, he stocked a supply of these new inventions.

After Mr Evans's death, the garage belonged to his widow, Mrs Ruth Evans (née Alp), and with the help of George's brother, Fred, they continued to run the garage and petrol pumps for many years.

20 Albert Neal: Steeplejack

Mr Albert (Alb) Neal spent his working life as a steeplejack. It was he who placed the weather vane on the steeple of Tetbury Church.

In later years Mr Neal had difficulty in walking, having to lift his legs high in the air with each step he took. His precarious job, and the many years he spent climbing steeples, was attributed to this complaint.

Below Left: Alb Neal outside his house at the Barton, 1930.

Below right: Mr & Mrs Chambers in the garden at the back of the New Inn, with their grandson, Arthur Palmer, 1942.

PUBLIC HOUSES

1 The New Inn

As the name implies, the New Inn became an ale house much later than the other public houses in the village.

In the 1920s Mr W Wilcox had his beer retailing business here. It was then taken over by Mr and Mrs Chambers who stayed until the mid-1940s. The last licensee at the New Inn was Mr Butler, who later changed the property back to a private house.

The New Inn sign proudly stated that — *All beers are drawn straight from the wood.*

The New Inn (extreme left) 1940; on its right is Miss Ball's sweet shop with a cigarette vending machine and an advertisement for Gold Flake tobacco on the wall.

2 The Rattlebone Inn

The Rattlebone Inn was built in the 17th century and occupied an important site, at the entrance to the old market place. Named in honour of the village hero, it is now one of the only two remaining public houses in the village.

For well over twenty-five years, Mr Frank Knapp was the landlord at the *Bones*. The original Rattlebone Inn sign now hangs in the village hall. When the brewery, Whitbread-Flowers, who owned the pub, decided to sell it, they donated the sign to the village. However, after several years as an antique shop, the Rattlebone re-opened, much to the delight of the people of Sherston, and once again John Rattlebone's image (though not the original sign) hangs above the door.

The Rattlebone Inn, c. 1920, in the foreground on the right. The old pub sign, which now hangs in the Village Hall, is just visible.

Opposite: Jack Amos standing at the entrance to the Angel Hotel in 1935. His hanging flower baskets are just visible. Mrs Amos provided lunch time snacks and afternoon teas. The property to the right was the Swan Commercial Hotel, and next to that was The Old Bell.

3 The Angel Hotel

The Angel Hotel is probably the oldest of the public houses that were once in Sherston, being built in the early part of the 16th century. In 1648 it was owned by Mrs Winifred Goodcheap (née Cowley) and her inscription stone is still on the front of the building.

In 1889 Mr Ralph Goulding was licensee, also running his carrier trade from there, going to Chippenham on Mondays and Fridays, and returning the same day.

It was at the Angel in the early 1920s that entertainment was provided, courtesy of Mr Harry Poole, and Poole's *Myrorama* of Malmesbury. A series of pictures depicting topical events, historic happenings, and scenery were painted on to revolving screens, and these were then shown to the audience in a tent at the back of the Angel. The first ever movies in Sherston!

In the mid-1930s Mr Jack Amos was landlord and it was he who decided that hanging flower baskets would look attractive at the Angel. Also tubs along the front with conifers stood next to the standpipe beside the wide entrance that originally allowed coaches to pass through to the courtyard and barn at the back.

The sign of the Angel still swings outside, but now it houses Sherston Software, a computer software company.

4 The Swan Commercial Hotel

Built in the late 16th century, the Swan Hotel was the largest of the public houses in Sherston. Situated in the High Street, between the Angel and the Old Bell, the main part of the building, together with a barn and stables, was in the Swan Barton.

At this time the Swan was the village Post House, with travellers and their coaches breaking their journeys here. In 1899 Mr Thomas Andrews ran the Sherston to Badminton station horse bus, departing promptly from the Swan at 10.30am on Mondays, Thursdays, and Saturdays. The horse bus could carry ten passengers inside, with four more on top with the luggage.

Mr Samuel Goodfield was the publican at the Swan in the 1890s. The Goodfield family continued to run the pub until the 1920s, when Mrs Sylvia Goodfield, the last in the family line, completed the family's connection.

It was at the Swan that village business took place, including the sale of properties, auctions, and business meetings. On the 28 November 1919 the Sherston Co-Operative Milling Society held their Annual General Meeting at the Swan and paid Mrs Goodfield the sum of five shillings for the use of the Conference Room and refreshments.

It was in one of the upstairs' rooms of the Swan that the village Whipping Post was found.

The Swan continued in business, being run by Mrs Minnie Goulding, but finally closed its doors to the public in about 1933.

Opposite: The High Street taken from the Church tower, 1920. The Swan Commercial Hotel is on the right, before the standpipe and with a projecting sign.

5 The Bell

The Bell House was built in the late 17th century. From about 1911 until it closed in the late 1930s, Mr Alfred Rice was the Licensee.

Mr Rice was a plasterer and tiler by trade, and whilst he carried out his work, Mrs Rice ran the beer house and off-licence. Inside the pub there was a long counter with slots cut for the different sized coins — farthings, ha'pennies, and pennies. The school children would often cross the road to the Bell at lunch time to purchase a bag of broken crisps, or buy a string of liquorice for a farthing, always placing their coins in the counter.

After the closure of the Bell, Mr Herbert Goulding opened his butcher's shop in the building. The pub sign of the Bell still swings above the shop window and it is still a butcher's shop.

6 Forester's Arms

The Forester's Arms, on the east side of the High Street, was built in 1710 and, like the Court House, has an elegant stone shell porch over the front doorway. Originally there were livery stables and tack rooms at the back of the house.

From 1911 Maurice Powell was the licensee as well as being the village well-sinker. In 1931 the landlord was Arthur Goulding who stayed there until Mr and Mrs Cooper took over in the late 1940s. Mrs Amos, whose husband Jack had run the Angel Hotel, then bought the Forester's Arms and continued to run it as a guest house for many years.

Doug Goulding, with his mother, outside the Forester's Arms, c. 1935.

7 The Carpenter's Arms

The Carpenter's Arms was built some time in the late 17th century. Mrs A Cooper was landlady there in 1914 since when the landlords have been Mr Brewer, Mr Albert V Purnell, Mr G Waples, and Mr G Grubb.

The Carpenter's Arms was renowned in the 1960s for its cider. Since it was a traditional ale and cider house, it was uncommon to see any ladies in the pub.

In the early 1900s the village notice board was displayed on the double doors outside the Carpenters.

It is now one of the two remaining public houses left in the village.

The Carpenter's Arms, c. 1905.

BUILDINGS & SITES OF INTEREST

1 The Rifle Range

The Rifle Range was originally a tithe barn which belonged to Sir George Holford of Westonbirt.

Sir George, who owned several other properties in the village, died in September 1926 aged sixty-six. He left the barn to the people of the village as a place of meeting, recreation, and instruction, and specified that it should be under the jurisdiction of the vicar, who, at that time, was the Reverend Walter Cecil Page. There were also six trustees appointed: Mr Roland Brinkworth, schoolmaster, Miss Alice Pickering, Miss Cecilia Platt, Miss Mary Anne Lewis, District Nurse, Mr Roy Willoughby Boothe MRCS LRCP – all of the parish of Sherston – and Mr Charles McQuillan of Rodbourne.

It is stated in the Charity Commissioners' report that, although the vicar would take all major decisions concerning the use of the building, it is not an ecclesiastical charity and that there should be no restrictions on its use.

As the name implies, one of the first uses of the building was for the practice of rifle shooting. The targets were marked out on a large slate that was attached to pulleys at one end of the room. There were many other occasions when the Rifle Range would be an ideal venue, such as wedding receptions, dances, football and cricket club presentations, and even as a place to see all the latest cinema releases.

Wessex Cinemas used the Rifle Range on Wednesday and Saturday evenings. The price of admission was one shilling and one and ninepence, with the performances being held at 5.15pm and 8.00pm. In June 1954 they showed such classics as Audie Murphy in *Duel at Silver Creek*, Randolph Scott in *The Last of the Mohicans*, and even *Old Mother Riley Meets the Vampire*.

The Rifle Range has always been used for fund raising events, and in April 1920 there was a Whist Drive and Fancy Dress dance held with the proceeds going to the Church heating fund. Doctor and Mrs Hoskyn acted as judges for the fancy dress competition and awarded first prize to Miss Ruth Alp as a Crimson Rambler, and second prize went to Mr George Platt as a Clown. Over £10 was raised during the evening, taking the heating fund to £142.

The Sherston Cricket Club's Presentation Dinner in 1935.

2 The Church House

The Church Land's deed box contained a large number of deeds for properties belonging to the Church, dating as far back as 1404. Amongst these deeds was one dated 25 March 1511, and related to the building of a church house. This house stands in the High Street, opposite the village school. The sizes given for the original house were 60 feet by 19 feet, with the inside height being 16 feet. In 1859 the east end of the house was rebuilt.

It was at the Church House every Whitsun that the Ale Feast took place. This feast was an opportunity to raise funds for the Church. The ale would be brewed and the bread baked before Whitsun, and while the ale lasted, all other ale houses in the village would be closed. Considering that at that time there were fifteen ale houses in Sherston, one can imagine the sizeable profit this would provide for the Church! The ale and the bread would be distributed by the church wardens and sidesmen, and would be accompanied by dancing and singing, and the enactment of plays in the High Street. There is no record of when the Ale Feast ended in Sherston, but tradition carried on in the form of the Trinity Monday fairs. Nowadays, this is replaced by the Boules and Carnival week that takes place every year in the High Street.

In the early part of the 18th century, the Church House was let by the church wardens as a Poor House.

In 1895 Mr Edmund Merchant lived there, and carried out his profession as village blacksmith; he was also a beer retailer, possibly at the Old Bell house next door to his forge. His two sons both carried on the tradition as blacksmiths, Arthur working from his father's forge, and Harry from his forge opposite the church in Church Street.

In 1903 the village Reading and Coffee rooms were at the Church House. Mr Dear, the school's headmaster, who lived at the Laurels next door, was the secretary. Other Committee members included Dr Hunt, Mr Cam, Mr Sainsbury, and Mr Selwood; Mrs Head was the caretaker.

At one of the committee meetings it was noted that the members would be glad to see more genuine 'reading' members and there must be many who, while not allured perhaps by the attractions of the Games room, would appreciate a quiet smoke of an evening over the daily newspapers, or one of the many magazines provided in the upstairs room.

Also at the Church House the Registrar of Births, Marriages, and Deaths would attend once a week.

Miss Gertrude Merchant also lived at the Church House until her death in 1954. In her youth she had been a nurse, and in later years wrote some wonderful poems about Sherston and local events.

Taken in the 1950s this view of the High Street shows (extreme right) Mr Herbert Goulding's butcher's shop, which at one time was The Bell public house. The double doors to the right led to Mr Arthur Merchant's forge. The next two buildings comprised the Church House.

Above: Butcher Goulding admiring sheep in Court Street, being taken by Alistair Neal to Farmer Newth's in Sopworth Lane. Butcher Goulding's shop was on the corner of Back Street and Court Street, before he moved to premises in the High Street.
In the background is one of Sherston's coaches parked by the garages. Mr Minett's shop can also be seen.

Left: Butcher Goulding standing outside his 'thunder-box' before its demolition in 1963.

Above: Nurse Gertrude Merchant, c. 1905.

Opposite: 'Sherston', by Miss Gertrude Merchant, 13th September, 1945.
Overleaf: John Rattlebone: Hero of Sherston, by Miss Gertrude Merchant.

SHERSTON

I've heard that up in Parliament,
And I'll tell you if you please,
They speak of model villages,
And Sherston's one of these.

The village stands upon a hill,
The streets are broad and long,
The houses quaint and rugged,
The buildings firm and strong.

The Church stands like a sentinel,
With architecture fine,
As if to guard its children,
Beauty in every line.

A battle church of *Holy Cross*,
It has stood the test of time,
We thank our God, through wars
and bombs,
It stands the same, sublime.

Through all the years of wars and scars,
No missile has defaced,
The wondrous beauty of our church,
Or stolen from its grace.

And visitors with seeing eye,
Look on the pillars grand,
And arches of this house of God,
And marvel as they stand.

I think through the centuries,
How blest the place doth seem,
To see preserved this Church,
Just as it's always been.

And there's a hero of the place,
To his memory there's an Inn,
Called after one John Rattlebone,
Who fought in ten sixteen.

And in the street the old Church House,
Doth strike the stranger's eye,
For the lovely Tudor windows,
Of the past and days gone by.

JOHN RATTLEBONE: HERO OF SHERSTON

Ther wur a mon as I heared on,
That telled me as ees name wur John,
And on tother zide o' 'e,
Wur Rattlebone, luk zee.

An eff you went down She'ston way,
You'd ear more about un I dessay,
Vor down there they be main proud o' 'e,
As I da thenk they ought ta be.

Vor eff you'd lived in ten zixteen,
A battle there you might a zeen,
Twur tween two men o' girt repute,
One called Ironside and one Canute.

John vought wi Ironside, I've been told,
And showed eeself both brave and bold,
Vor 'e wur wounded thur wone day,
But 'e wurn't a fellow ta turn away.

John never knewed when he wur bate,
A capital chap ta battle wi fate,
Thic wound wur in ees stomach zee,
Zoe 'e clapped a tile stoan awver 'e.

And went on vighten, who but 'e,
As brave, as brave, as brave could be.
That's why they be zo proud of 'e,
Down at She'ston, dunne zee.

The children taught at mother's knee,
All about un hullucky,
And in the grand ol' church you'll zee,
A chest they zed belonged at 'e.

In Parvise of the Church twur thought,
John spent the night awore 'e rought,
Ther wur a coat o' mail as well,
But what's become on't I caint tell.

An thay beant gwain to vorget un neither,
Tha can allus drenk ta un in beer an cider,
Vor they named a Inn right a'ter 'e,
An ess thur vorright by thick Jubilee tree.

An on thic zign you can zee is John,
A zoldier like a courages mon,
Wi tile stoan, sword, an armoured zuit,
As wen ta battle ag'inst Canute.

3 The Jubilee Tree

The Jubilee Tree, situated on a triangle of grass opposite the Church, was donated and planted by Sir George Holford to celebrate the Diamond Jubilee of Queen Victoria in 1897. Sir George owned and planted nearby Westonbirt Arboretum.

Above: The Jubilee Tree, 1905;
Below: Mr & Mrs Tom Pritchard, of Noble Street, c. 1920; seen here with two cartloads of material for use in his trade as hurdle-maker. He was also a coal merchant.

4 Noble Street

The row of houses in the photograph above were built in the mid-seventeenth century, approximately. One evening in 1961, for no apparent reason, they collapsed.

It was at Number 8 Noble Street in November 1925 that a tragedy occurred to Mrs Louisa Pritchard, wife of Thomas Pritchard, who was a coal merchant. Mr Pritchard had left home at 8.30am that morning to go to Hullavington Station to collect coal. On his return journey he was met by Walter Wilcox, who informed him that his wife had suffered a 'giddy turn' whilst cooking, and had fallen near the fire. With her clothes alight, she rushed outside where the wind fanned the fire, engulfing Mrs Pritchard in a mass of flames.

Mr Harold Bonner, a farmer and dairyman, who lived at Number 1 Noble Street, was in his yard when he heard terrible screams and saw Mrs Pritchard running towards him, her clothing ablaze. He ran back into his house, grabbed a rug, and threw it around her to smother the flames.

Despite Doctor Langton Butler's and the District Nurse's prompt action, Mrs Pritchard had received dreadful burns to her whole body and sadly died at 9.00pm that same evening. She was 74 years old.

5 The Tolsey

In 1511 Sherston was greatly reduced in size due to a fire which destroyed most of its buildings. The village's timber-framed houses, exposed position, and distance from water would all have contributed to this devastation.

Until this time, Sherston had been a thriving market town with a market being held every Friday in the wide High Street. It was to the Tolsey, or Market House, that the traders would go to pay their market tolls. It was also the venue for the merchants and leaders of the townsmen to meet for their discussions on trade regulations. Beside the Tolsey stood the village stocks and one of the market crosses.

In 1922, Mr Joe Bignell, who was a carpenter and builder in the village, purchased the old Tolsey buildings, which by then had been altered and converted to three cottages. Due to their bad state of repair, Joe decided to demolish them and rebuild on the site. He had many ideas for the building that was to be built, ranging from a cinema, bus depot, where repairs could be made to the Bristol bus which ran daily through the village, and even a gymnasium. However, only the shell of the building was erected before Joe died.

The building then stood vacant for many years until it was bought by the Youth Hostel Association. Showers were installed upstairs, partitions were erected to provide sleeping accommodation, and for many years members of the YHA used the Tolsey for overnight stays whilst on their bicycle trips.

During the war years, the Army commandeered the building as quarters for the men guarding prisoners-of-war who were detained in Sherston.

In June 1949 the members of the British Legion in Sherston were asked whether they would be willing to make a donation or loan to raise the deposit needed to purchase the Tolsey. Until then the 100 members and their President, Colonel Keith Menzies, had had nowhere permanent to meet.

The deposit was found and for many years the rooms were full of ex-Servicemen. Snooker tables were installed for their entertainment. The Football Club hired the changing rooms and showers, and together with funds raised from letting rooms on the top floor for Whist and Beetle drives, the Legion was able to maintain the building and provide assistance to ex-Servicemen and women in the village.

Since then, the Tolsey has had many uses, including the storage of antiques, building materials, a print shop, offices, and currently it is the doctors' surgery.

Sherston High Street, 1905, looking north. In the foreground, on the right, are the Tolsey cottages which, by this time, had become considerably dilapidated, particularly the roofs. Mr Henry Merchant, whose blacksmith's forge was at the end of the row of houses, can here be seen at work.

The Court House at the junction of Back and Court Streets, 1905.

6 The Court House, Court Street

The Court House is situated at the junction of Back Street and Court Street. It was built in the early part of the 16th century, and rebuilt in the latter part of the same century.

The original Court House incorporated the two houses on the corner of Back Street and Court Street. At the front entrance of the house is an elegant stone shell canopy over the front door, reputedly one of the best examples in the country. There were also vaulted lock-ups in the basement.

It was at the Court House that the Lord of the Manor held his Court Leets, and imposed appropriate fines and punishments for crimes committed in the village.

In 1880 the Court House, and the row of houses adjoining it to the right, became the general warehouse, whose proprietor was Mr Clement Palser. He employed seven people who also lodged at the premises. These shop assistants came from as far afield as Cork in Ireland, London, and Humberside.

In 1904 Mr Johnny Minett purchased the warehouse, and changed the name to Court House Stores, where the Minett family continued to run the business until the late 1950s.

7 Balcony House

The Balcony House, situated on the west side of the High Street, is reputed to be the oldest house in Sherston, and was one of the few buildings to survive the fire of 1511. The original house was built in the middle part of the 14th century, with further rebuilding being carried out in the 17th century.

In 1705 Queen Anne stayed at the Balcony House whilst on her way to *take the Waters* at Bath.

In the cellars beneath the front of the house there is still visible the blocked up entrances to a tunnel which supposedly runs from the cliff, under the High Street, and into the Church.

In 1939 Mr and Mrs Bourne ran Ye Olde Balconee Guest House. It then became the Balcony Shop, but is now a private residence.

8 The Church Lych-Gate

The Church lych-gate forms the entrance to the Churchyard. Originally built in the 17th century, it was altered and repaired in 1920.

It now serves as a war memorial to the men from Sherston who laid down their lives in the Great War of 1914-18. These men were Algernon Neal, Reginald Rice, Herbert Neal, William Brakespear, Verney Neal, William Evans, Walter Palmer, Thomas Dickenson, James Berry, Edward Sainsbury, Archibald Merchant, Robert Jeffery, William Price, James Berry, Arthur Jobbins, Charlie Neal, H Alp, Daniel Niblet, James Ponting, and Frederick Saunders.

Sherston Branch of the Royal British Legion on parade, Remembrance Sunday 1967.
Front Row (l-r): Herbie Butler, Gordon Sainsbury (Standard bearer), Herbie Long.
2nd row: Graham Goulding, Walt (Mackie) Bishop, Butcher Goulding.
Behind (l-r): Ivor Jobbins, Abbie Berry, Ron Purnell, Percy Neal, Billy (Winkle) Neal, Jim Stiles, Colonel Grant-Thorold, Colonel Renton.
Scouts: Rodney Butler, John Butler; Scout Leader: Derek James.

'Greater love hath no man than this, that a man lay down his life for his friends.'